THE COMPLETE BOOK OF

combat systema

I dedicate this book to my father, Royal Secours, for having taught me the meaning of honor, and to my son, Reza Secours, for teaching me the meaning of joy.

Kevin Secours

THE COMPLETE BOOK OF

combat systema

Paladin Press • Boulder, Colorado

Other titles by Kevin Secours:

Combat Systema, Vol. 1: The Russian Martial Art of Hand-to-Hand Combat (video)
Combat Systema, Vol. 2: The Russian Martial Art of Armed Combat (video)
Combat Systema, Vol. 3: The Russian Martial Art of Ground Combat (video)
Combat Systema, Vol. 4: The Russian Martial Art of Impact Striking (video)

The Complete Book of Combat Systema
by Kevin Secours

Copyright © 2016 by Kevin Secours
ISBN 13: 978-1-61004-892-7
Printed in the United States of America

Published by Paladin Press, a division of
Paladin Enterprises, Inc.
P.O. Box 1307
Boulder, CO 80306 USA
+1.303.443.7250

Direct inquiries and/or orders to the above address.

Visit our website at www.paladin-press.com.

C O N T E N T S

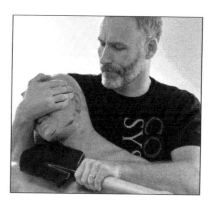

ACKNOWLEDGMENTS

- Special thanks to Combat Systema practitioners and instructors worldwide. Your continuing support and passion improve me daily.
- I would also like to thank the following Combat Systema actors/students featured in the photos:

  Sébastien Lebeau (the main model)
  Giordano Watkins
  Anthony Donovan
  Gabriel Lemay
  Darren Egoyan
  Joseph Kam

- Thank you to Alexandrina Delage for her tireless assistance in structuring, editing, and photographing this book. I could not have done this without you.
- Thank you to my many teachers past and present for letting me stand on your shoulders. I carry your teachings with me in every minute of my life.

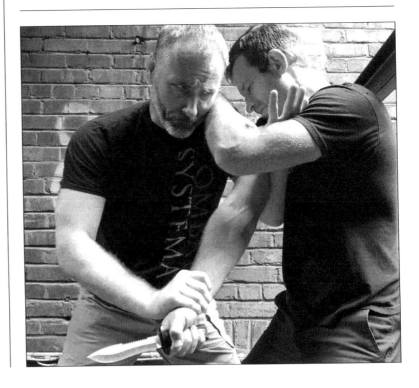

PREFACE

WHERE COMBAT SYSTEMA COMES FROM

In 1998 while we were changing after a kali training session, a friend of mine held up a videocassette and asked, "You ever seen the Russian martial arts?"

I shook my head as he passed it to me. Looking at the label to read the name of the video, I realized it was in Cyrillic. The sweat on my hand was starting to make the ink on the homemade label run. "Any good?" I asked as I tried to blot it on the only dry patch I could find on my pant leg.

"It's interesting," he replied. "Weird as hell but interesting."

Little did I know that the tape I tucked into my bag and forgot about for a few days would be my introduction to a 16-year (and counting) journey into the unorthodox world of the Russian martial arts.

Most people don't realize that Russia even has its own martial arts. The usual questions about Russian martial arts abound:

- Are they a fusion of jujitsu and karate?
- Are they like Krav Maga?
- From which styles are they compiled?

You're forgiven for immediately conjuring images of shaolin monks and board-breaking karateka when you think of the martial arts. Thank you, Hollywood. In reality, most cultures that have survived for any significant time have needed to develop their approach to combat. A country as huge as Russia has a wide variety of indigenous arts.

While the Russian martial arts are not a hybrid, they are heavily influenced by the martial arts of many cultures. Russia is an enormous country with a huge border that was challenged by a long history of invasion and occupation. Between the 13th and 15th centuries alone, the country endured more than 160 wars. Consequently, the Russians were constantly exposed to exotic weapons and strategies. The massive variety of geography inside Russia also meant that tactics needed to be adaptable to changing conditions, and that's a big part of why the traditional Russian martial arts are so free and playful.

Some of the oldest records, dating back to the 13th century, refer to cultural traditions of bare-knuckle boxing. These methods of fisticuffs featured heavily in festivals and religious celebrations. Variations include the art of Skobar, which was practiced in the territory of the union of East Slavic tribes known as the Krivichi. Original variations included combat with sticks and then later evolved to safer empty-handed variations. Over time, social norms evolved to make competitions safer, and conventions were established eliminating kicks, throws with the legs, and strikes to felled opponents. Combat could take place between individuals or between large groups numbering in the hundreds, where individuals would crash into each other like avalanches. Battles would commonly be waged between the citizens of different streets, villages, or districts. Music often played a significant role in these endeavors, with fighters entering a trancelike state from the rhythm. The musicians could also signal the halt of a fight by stopping the music.

Fighting often included primitive stomping of the feet, beating of the chest, and loud whooping or cheering, which were believed to cultivate the vital energy, or "yar," of the opponent. Force was thought to originate in the solar plexus and to shift to the lunar plexus (navel) and back, creating a buoyant quality in the movement that utilized low, plunging squats and elastic lunges and springing steps that could be used to stomp the feet and trap an opponent's legs. Since fighting was usually done in groups, tactics generally favored striking quickly and fluidly in multiple directions. This led to a fluid figure-eight motion with the arms that allowed practitioners to move smoothly from one target to another, freely interchanging their hands and elbows.

The uniqueness of the Russian arts stems from the uniqueness of the country itself. Many scholars consider Russia the center of a distinct Orthodox civilization. It starts with Russia's Byzantine parentage, its distinct religion, 200 years of Tatar rule, and, perhaps most important, Russia's limited exposure to the Renaissance, Reformation, and Enlightenment, which were central Western experiences.[1] Like Japan, Russia also resisted the onslaught of European expansion due in large part to a highly centralized imperial government that allowed them to maintain an independent existence.

After the Russian Revolution in 1917, the global climate shifted dramatically. The days of the world being dominated by conflicts between nation-states gave rise to conflicts between ideologies. It began with wars between fascism, communism, and liberal democracy. During the Cold War, these ideologies were embodied by the leading superpowers, which set the stage for the world that we live in today. That conflict was also the forge that refined the Russian martial arts into their modern form. In anticipation of global warfare, the Soviet government commissioned combat researchers to travel throughout the world to study different approaches. They tested these methods and integrated the best concepts with their own native traditions. This

1.   Huntington, Samual P., *The Clash of Civilizations and the Remaking of World Order* (Sydney: Simon and Schuster, Inc., 1996).

period of development led to the creation of distinct Soviet martial arts, including Sport Sambo, Combat Sambo, and Samoz, which was later modified and became known simply as Systema (literally "the System"). After the fall of the Soviet Union, ex-soldiers began migrating throughout the world, slowly spreading these approaches.

What I saw on that video my friend lent me was definitely "weird as hell but interesting." There were guys diving through fire, throwing military shovels, and shooting blindfolded. It showed mobility exercises unlike anything I had ever seen. There was also a lot of stuff that immediately set off my bunk detector, such as psychic energy work and touchless nonsense that I assumed was propaganda material. It took me years of high-level training to make sense of it all and to navigate through the clutter.

In the following pages, I will share the very best of it with you. Be warned: I have no interest in being a curator of Russian traditions. I am not here to preserve traditional ways or to be a Russophile. I am unabashedly a Westerner, and I will be giving you a most Western perspective of my experience. I will highlight what worked for me. I will tell you how it changed my life and show you how to use it to dramatically improve yours. I will also be the first to highlight the mysticism, flag the BS, and keep things practical, provable, and profitable for your health and survival.

INTRODUCTION

GOVERNING BELIEFS

I wrote this manual based on a few governing beliefs. First, I believe that combative training should enhance your quality of life and health. Each of us may face violence in our lives with varying degrees of probability. If you are a soldier, law enforcement officer, or doorman at a club or bar, the probability is high. If you are a civilian, the likelihood is probably much lower. We invest in training methods that we believe will improve our odds of survival. This is what I term our "calculus of violence"—how much are we willing to risk in our training versus what we estimate we will get in return? Once I thought that preparing for violence needed to be violent. Now I believe that there is no logic in forsaking the health and joy you initially set out to preserve in your training.

I would also submit that it isn't necessary to risk your safety. K. Anders Ericsson at Florida State University found through his research that, in the vast majority of cases, talent is forged, not innate at birth.[1]

Save a few exceptional characteristics like smallness for a jockey or height for a basketball player, the greatest amount of variance in expert performers comes from intense amounts of effort and practice. Ericsson also found that the intense amount of practice required to achieve mastery demands the extreme motivation that can only come from loving the process. Enjoyment breeds repetition, and motivation and joy are far more likely and sustainable from training that cultivates an overall feeling of health. Nothing destroys dedication or disrupts training like injuries. Safer training is more likely to achieve excellence than reckless training.

Deeply connected to this idea of healthy training is the notion of improving body intelligence, awareness, and grace. Modern life usually demands only very rudimentary competence in our bodies. If we have basic balance, basic mobility and basic awareness, we can get through traffic, survive school or the office, and get back home again in time for supper; little more body awareness is required for the modern masses. Those few rare individuals who do crack through this tedium and expand their physical capacities are revered as sacred reminders of our inherent capacities. Consider the value we bestow on elite athletes.

I believe that we are entitled to more than this. In our training, we must not be content to quietly accept a loss of our potential. We must not simply accept that we must brutalize our bodies and pay the price down the road to gain combative skills. We deserve much more. We are entitled to greater health, improved mobil-

ity, a surging strength, and a graceful ease and confidence in our days. Combative training that engenders these feelings is self-motivating. The power and energy that issue forth from a general feeling of vitality are unbounded. As wellness and the self-awareness that accompanies it increase, we become not only more capable of defending ourselves, but also less likely to be victimized in the first place as we ascend from the timid ranks of the aged, the meek, the distracted, and the weak whom predators typically target.

A final governing belief is the idea that training must be pressure-tested. Donald Meichenbaum created the idea of stress inoculation at the University of Waterloo, where it was noted that successful preparation for surviving stress requires three basic criteria. First there is an education phase, wherein the subject identifies the goals of the exercise. Simply put, you need to know why you are doing what you are doing. Then there is the rehearsal phase, where the subject explores the drill and gains basic competence. Finally, there is the stress phase, wherein pressure is incrementally added so that the subject has to struggle to succeed. Struggle, more than simple repetition, is what bolsters accelerated learning. In fact, the subject may even fail more than he succeeds, providing he stops the pressure at some point and restarts the cycle, debriefing what worked and what didn't, setting modified goals, and then rehearsing the new skill. This simple formula is my training mantra. It must support the previous pillars, and things must be kept safe and healthy; ultimately, students must walk out with greater awareness and mindfulness. But there must be pressure to distill the nonsense from the gems.

Let's get into it.

1. Ericsson, K. Anders, Ralph Kramne, and Clemens Tesch-Romer, "The Role of Deliberate Practice in the Acquisition of Expert Performance," *Psychological Review*, Vol. 100, No.3 (1993): 363–406.

S E C T I O N

1

"Good enough will always be the enemy of perfection."
—Mikhail Kalashnikov

FOUNDATION

VISUALIZATION

Take a moment to imagine someone who is an elite performer. I'm talking about a true professional at the very top of his game. This could be an athlete, a pilot, a special ops soldier, a doctor, or a scientist. Choose the first elite performer that comes to mind and visualize that person.

EXERCISE 1
VISUALIZE EXCELLENCE

Deeply see your subject as he performs his chosen mastery. How does his posture look? How does he move? What does the expression on his face look like? Observe the characteristics of his coordination, grace, and mastery as if you were feeling that same ease and confidence and sharing his skill. Now, imagine how that individual started out. Was he naturally adept? Did things come easily to him? Did he work less hard than everyone else and just seem to grasp things automatically?

Before you answer, let's approach this another way:

• If you threw up the first time you flew in a plane, would that mean you were never meant to be a pilot? Ace Eddie Rickenbacker was America's most successful pilot in World War I. He overcame a fear of heights, an eye injury, and a habit of routinely vomiting from airsickness to earn 26 air victories. How did he do it? It started by him wanting to fly so badly that he falsified documents to enlist when he was underage. Then he volunteered for high-risk missions that no one else would take and flew in combat every chance he got. He knew that struggle can make skill.

• If you were a horrible shot the first time you fired a gun, would you just accept that was your lot in life and abandon any hopes for elite precision? In what is likely a bit of an exaggeration, SEAL Team 6 founder Richard Marcinko claimed that his unit used more ammo than the entire U.S. Marine Corps. Through extensive practice, his SEALs established a standard of being able to shoot a 3x5-inch index card at 30 feet. They didn't come in natural-born shooters—they made themselves into them.

• Can you imagine ever becoming so good that you could just stop learning? Dr. Michael E.

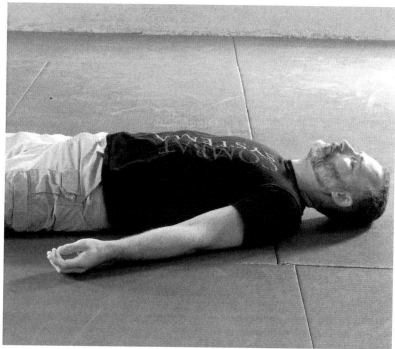

DeBakey was still considered the guru of cardiac surgeons when he died in 2008 at the age of 99. DeBakey never stopped learning. From his childhood onward, he was driven to constantly innovate. As a surgeon, he pioneered new approaches and created new equipment, performing more than 60,000 surgeries in his lifetime. His mastery was hard earned and fueled by his love. He never stopped improving.

Now let me ask you again: do you think that the elite performer you selected was born that way and just stepped into his destined role, or did he dedicate countless hours, repeating, refining, and improving himself until he became the master performer you imagined? The simple truth is that no one is born ready-made for excellence. As Miyamoto Musashi said, mastery is a constant journey. It's doubtful anyone actually achieves it, but we know that the right type of hard work can forge excellence. Regardless of what your current skill level is today as you are reading this, you have the capacity to get better—to get much better. What would you like to achieve?

Imagine that you are sitting in a comfortable cinema watching a large screen. Feel the seat under your body. Let yourself become completely relaxed in that seat. On the screen, you are watching a film about you, about your ideal you. This is the you that you wish to become—free of injuries, in control of your fears, graceful and confident.

- What do you look like?
- How are you standing?
- How are you moving?

Imagine that you are actually on that screen. How does it feel to be in this state of mastery? Take a moment to plant a seed of that feeling in your memory. We will be coming back to the feeling of mastery shortly.

EXERCISE 2
PUTTING THE SELF IN SELF-DEFENSE

Mastery is possible. Yes, it takes hard work, but the good news is that there are tons of im-

mediate and short-term rewards along the way to keep you motivated. We'll be getting to those in a few pages. Before we can get there, however, we need to reinforce our basic motivation. While motivation is obviously essential in having the perseverance to achieve that mastery over the long term, it's also vital in your short-term training. The reason *why* you are training will determine the type of techniques and strategies you choose. The motivation to win in a sport will lead you to choose different tactics and methods than the motivation to survive a life and death fight would.

The first step in bolstering your motivation is to take a quick inventory of what you value. Take a minute to think of everything you love, like, and enjoy. Absolutely anything can be on this list—your family, friends, pets, and favorite places, foods, songs, and movies. Think of literally everything that you enjoy in your life without any specific judgment or order. Thinking of your favorite song before you think of a member of your family doesn't necessarily reflect what you love more and, even if it did, it doesn't matter. Let that list churn and populate freely for a minute.

Now take a second to recognize that all those items on that list are unique to you. Did you list yourself? If so, were you the first thing

you thought of? Were you at the top of the list? If you weren't, you're not alone. Most people don't put themselves there. In any case, we need to put ourselves at the top of the list now. Visualize yourself writing your name on the very top of that list. Your unique relationship to everything that you listed on your value inventory is the reason why you are training. That list is unique to you. No one else has exactly those experiences or likes and loves. When we train to defend ourselves, we are training to protect everything that list represents. Your motive matters more than any method you choose to follow. The reason *why* you are training matters much more than *how* you are training.

Now that we know the level of mastery we're aiming for and we've bolstered our essential motivation to go forward, it's time to fill in the gaps.

THE SPINAL ENGINE

In the words of Professor Serge Gracovetsky, the spine is the engine of all movement. When we look at the role the spine plays in animals like snakes or fish, it's quite apparent that movement occurs in their spines, but when we look at humans, people tend to prioritize the importance of the legs. However, the reality is that the legs are little more than a support structure for our spines. A human without legs is still able to generate movement, hobble on the hips, roll over, or move in other ways. If we look at a newborn infant, we see the evolution of movement in his learning cycle. First, children learn to lift their head and then their shoulders; then they master rolling over and finally sitting up unsupported before ever incorporating their limbs and learning to crawl or pull themselves up to a standing position. We learn to move from the spine outward.

If you view your spine from the side, it has a natural S-curve composed of three arches. First the neck dips in at the cervical arch, second it curves out slightly at the shoulders from the thoracic arch, and, third, it slopes back inward in the lower back with the lumbar arch. This counterbalance works like a spring to absorb shock. Daily stress, injuries, and chronic tension deform these arches and rob the spine of its full capacity.

EXERCISE 3
THE SPINAL CHECK

To begin to optimize the incredible power in your spine, simply lie down flat on your back or sit comfortably in a chair. Keep your arms and legs uncrossed and positioned naturally. Take a breath and bring your awareness to how and where your back is touching the ground or the back of your chair.

- If the back of your body were rolled in ink, what type of imprint would you be making right now? Does it feel like you would be making a symmetrical image?
- Are both of your shoulder blades touching evenly?
- Is your nose pointed directly to the centerline of your body?
- Are your ears the same distance from either shoulder?
- Are your hands resting in the same position?
- Are your toes pointed at the same angle?

Take a moment to shift and adjust anything you need to improve your symmetry.

- First, imagine that there is a small thread running from the center of your crown. Feel that thread gently pulling your head away from your shoulders. As your neck elongates, softly tuck your chin toward your body. This tuck should be very slight, almost invisible. This simple adjustment helps improve your cervical arch.
- Second, gently raise your shoulders up toward your ears a fraction of an inch and then softly squeeze the shoulder blades together. If you are lying on the ground, feel the natural space this creates between your spine and the ground. If you are seated, feel the weight of your arms hanging comfortably from your shoulder frame. This shift helps improve your thoracic arch.

An example of bad posture.

Neck check.

Shoulder check.

- Finally, curl your tailbone forward and then up slightly, as you simultaneously pull your ribs in toward your spine. This will give your abdomen and lower back a solid, braced feeling but should not be done so strongly that it interferes with full, natural breaths.

Remember this feeling of alignment and strength. You have already moved one step closer toward that posture of confidence and grace that you visualized in Exercise 1. We will return to this feeling often through our physical work and will continuously check and reset our spinal alignment in this way throughout our training and our day-to-day life.

Tailbone check.

EXERCISE 4
THE COMBAT SYSTEMA SQUAT

It's time to stress-test our spinal alignment. Stand up with your feet shoulder-width apart. Take three small consecutive jumps without judgment or thought and then freeze. Take a look at the position of your feet.

- Did your feet move closer together or wider apart?
- Are your feet parallel?

If the spacing of your feet has changed, reposition them roughly shoulder-width again. See if you can comfortably move your feet into a parallel position. If there is any pain, particularly in the knees, you can allow your toes to point outward slightly, providing that the angle is symmetrical in both feet. Do not allow the toes to point inward.

- From this position, perform your spinal check, elongating your nape, subtly tucking your chin, rolling your shoulders up and slightly back, and, most important, curling the tailbone under as you pull the ribs gently in toward the spine.
- From this braced position, slowly begin squatting, being sure to keep your heels on the floor and your knees aligned over your arches. If you honestly keep your tailbone contracted, you will notice that you can only squat a few inches before you feel like you have hit a floor of tension. If you keep your tailbone contracted, you will not be able to go down any farther.
- Now slowly begin releasing your tailbone as you continue through this floor. Stop your squat a few inches below your tension floor once you have fully released your tailbone. At this new height, you will notice that you are unable to curl the tailbone back inward.

Front starting position for feet-parallel Combat Systema squat.

Side view of starting position.

Stop at your tension floor.

Releasing tailbone.

A full-plunge Combat Systema squat.

- Reverse the movement, slowly rising up while constantly curling inward with the tailbone. It will feel as if the tailbone were pushing you up.

This simple exercise helps to reinforce the role of the spine as the engine of movement. It also helps us compare the feeling of a braced spine with the tailbone under in a higher position versus a released tailbone in a low position. A correct engagement of the spine will be essential in remaining safe, healthy, and injury free in all of our training. It will be integral to correct power generation, and it will be vital when it's time to absorb impact.

THE POWER OF THE PIVOT

Poor body mechanics are all around us. A lack of body awareness and coordination routinely robs people of their potential power, blocking them with needless contraction before they can generate it or else leaking it out of their structure through instability. At my school and through my various seminars, I have had the fortune of training thousands of individuals over the past decades. One of the biomechanical weaknesses I encounter the most is poor pivoting skills. Aside from stifling potential, a failure to pivot correctly also places your body at immense risk of injury.

EXERCISE 5
THE PERFECT PIVOT

Begin by standing like you would to perform a Combat Systema squat—feet shoulder-width and symmetrical, spine braced and balanced. Now gently begin pushing your feet apart as if you were trying to rip the ground apart between them. Be careful not to allow your feet to roll outward on their blades or allow your knees to lean outward past your feet. Maintain good alignment, almost as if you were trying to push outward and pull inward at the same time. This state is often referred to as "biotensegrity." Initially, it is far better to exaggerate the contraction. You can reduce it gradually and refine your sensitivity as you progress.

A pivot consists of two parts—the framing foot and the pivoting foot. Both must remain solidly connected to the ground. The framing foot must stay balanced over the arch without rolling onto the outer blade. The pivoting foot must stay solidly on the ball of the foot without lifting up onto the tiptoes, flipping over onto the instep, or, worse still, losing contact with the ground. By maintaining this solid contact, you are able to push off against the ground and direct that power toward your target.

Close-up of standing position.

You can't practice the pivot enough. Simple bodyweight squats a few inches lower than your comfort zone can accelerate your practice, as can holding equal-sized weights in each hand or carrying a partner on your back to add load.

The correct way to perform the pivot.

Two examples of bad pivot: (top) losing contact with the floor and (bottom) flipping onto the instep.

PLASTICITY

"Men are born soft and supple; dead they are stiff and hard. Plants are born tender and pliant; dead, they are brittle and dry. Thus whoever is stiff and inflexible is a disciple of death. Whoever is soft and yielding is a disciple of life. The hard and stiff will be broken. The soft and supple will prevail."
—Laozi (also Lao-tzu), 6th century B.C.

Imagine you were standing in front of Mike Tyson in his prime. He is furious with you because of a misunderstanding. You are unarmed. He swings a power hook at your head. Would you rather block it or get out of the way?

Blocking, no matter how soft or fluid, still seeks to stop incoming force directly. Sometimes, there is no choice and blocking is better than taking a shot to the head, but too many styles promote and volunteer for a force-on-force mentality. Think of a huge guy, jacked up on HGH and steroids, with muscles bulging through his T-shirt, with distorted veins that look like gummy worms. On top of this, he's the type of guy who has a permanent frown on his face and walks through life looking for a fight. If you accidentally brush shoulders with this guy on a busy street, you are likely to get jolted by a hard shoulder hit and an angry stare, and suddenly there is a high risk of escalation. Now think of another guy: he can still be huge and fit, but he is loose, smiling, at peace with the world. This person is slipping through the crowd like a dancer. If you accidentally bump into him, there is nothing there. You slip past and continue.

The goal of the Combat Systema practitioner is to yield and evade like that second example. Certainly, there are still times when blocking is your only choice, but even the way you block can be soft and yielding like Muhammad Ali's "rope-a-dope" or spastic and overly tense like an awkward new student. It's up to you to set your goal. The most essential drill for cultivating this softness in Combat Systema is so simple that it's often taken for granted. So, I will preface by saying that the complexity of an idea does not determine its worth. Be careful not to underestimate this one. I urge you to include the following drill for five minutes in your daily training.

EXERCISE 6
THE PUSH 'N' YIELD DRILL

Stand in front of your training partner. Begin extremely slowly and take turns reaching, touching, and pushing each other. The goal of the recipient is to let the push move him. This sounds much easier than it actually is because many people tense up in anticipation. They freeze and fight the push, or even try to anticipate the push and in doing so often move the wrong way into the oncoming force. The more nervous you are, the more likely this is to happen, so I am speaking specifically to you guys when I say, slow down. It is impossible to respond too slowly on this drill. Push each other slowly and deeply, and let the push move you.

The first thing that will happen in most cases is that people will think so much about yielding that this becomes its own form of tension. The only way through this overthinking is to just keep on doing it nonstop for five minutes. Push each other back and forth. Talk about something you watched on TV last night to get your brain off the drill. Get in a few hundred pushes. Slowly, your body will take over and start responding.

Once you get into the flow, the next consideration is to return to that spinal balance and awareness you cultivated in Exercise 3. Remember that ideal posture is relative to context.

Rather than trying to impose a perfect everyday posture on the fight, let yourself be deformed and moved. The goal is not to impose an artificial upright posture in a crisis situation. Instead, understand how force deforms your structure, how you can acquire the best structure possible to endure each stressor, and how you can get back to ideal structure when it is safely possible.

One interesting guideline you can apply to this work is to be conscious of how you are yielding. Sometimes when you are quite balanced, you will be able to move with the force as one solid piece, maintaining the structure of your body during the evasion. For example, if I push you squarely in the sternum, you are likely to just step back without much deformation. Other times, the force will intersect your body on an angle that requires you to yield more with one section of your body. For example, if I stab at your groin, you are more likely to snap your hips back first rather than step back with your feet and move as a whole. Both types of yielding are ends of the same spectrum and essential to survival. Try becoming conscious of when you are able to move as a whole and when and what makes you move just a part. When you do move only one section of your body, return to a balanced and full structure as soon as you safely can. Do not volunteer to become out of balance or dwell there.

Starting position for push-and-yield drill.

Yielding to contact.

Yielding to second push to the hip.

Example of yielding with part—just the shoulder.

Example of yielding as a whole—stepping back.

EXERCISE 7
ADVANCED YIELDING

This simple yielding drill can be adapted dozens of ways. Here are a couple of options:

• Get into a squat, push-up, or sit-up position face-to-face with a partner. Practice taking turns, slowly pushing each other while hold-

ing the position. For a harder challenge, try yielding while performing reps. Then evolve to starting off side by side.

• Try performing the same drill while lying on the ground or standing against a wall. Now instead of retreating with the part of your body that is touched, you will need to advance with the opposite side of your body.

Facing a partner in a squat.

Yielding in the squat.

Yielding in a static sit-up.

Sit-up yielding continued.

Yielding on the ground.

Feeling direction of force.

Lifting the free part of the body.

Evading the force completely.

THE THREE FRAMES

As I noted, evading is not always enough. You certainly still need to deflect and block. Combat Systema advocates three basic types of defense for the upper body:

- Lower frames are when the arms are hanging naturally at your side. Through the rotation of your torso and a proper pivot, you can produce a natural deflection, like an elephant swinging its trunk.

- Middle frames are when the hands are held roughly around chest height and the elbows are raised, dropped, or circled like wings to deflect or block.

- Upper frames are when the hands are up near or on top of the head. Deflections occur in a motion that is akin to washing your hair. Refer to the following page.

Lower frame.

Lower-frame deflection.

Lower-frame close-up.

Middle frame.

Middle-frame deflection.

The key to successful deflections is that the hands and arms are kept close to the body as if you were wiping yourself rather than overextending and reaching for the attack, which would leave you vulnerable. A second characteristic is that yielding is prioritized and your evasive movement creates the deflection as a natural counterbalance.

Upper frame.

Upper-frame deflection.

EXERCISE 8
INCORPORATING DEFLECTIONS

- Return to the previous yielding drill. To best isolate the use of the lower frame, restrict pushes to the torso area. Begin with your arms hanging in a natural position. Again, wait for contact, allowing the push to move you. As you yield on contact, allow the natural motion of your arm to create a deflection. Initially, try to see how much the arm moves by virtue of the evasion alone. Then, slowly add the slightest amount of energy to the deflection to ensure that the arm contacts the attacker's arm at some level with the forearm, humerus, or shoulder. Always prioritize adding the least amount of energy and working close to the body.

Start facing your partner.

Contact on torso, feeling direction of force.

Moving with force.

Evasion creates natural deflection.

- Repeat the drill (below) with the arms in middle frame. When lifting the elbow, keep the motion loose and circular. Allow the elbow to drop back down to a natural resting position after the deflection to help keep the muscles loose and responsive. To best isolate this frame, focus on pushes aimed at chest level.

- Perform the drill (below) a third time, with the hand in upper frame. Keep pushes aimed at the shoulders and face. In addition to imitating the action of washing the hair and rotating the torso, it is helpful to keep the legs springy and to bob up and down slightly to assist deflection.

Middle-frame contact.

Middle-frame deflection.

Contact to the face.

Upper-frame deflection.

UNDERSTANDING DISTANCE

A key component in evasion is your understanding and control of distance. As we discussed earlier, as children we learn to move from the spine first and then progress outward to the limbs. In exactly this way, we started reeducating our ability to evade aggression by absorbing with the trunk first to allow the body to understand the movement in the spine. Then we evolved to include the arms to deflect. The next step is to progress to moving preemptively. The danger here is that you begin to rush and forget the previous steps. Work slowly at first and monitor your actions, being careful not to prioritize arm movement without clearing the line of attack with your body.

EXERCISE 9
MOVING PREEMPTIVELY

Return to the previous yielding drill. Begin in the same way, waiting for the pushes to move you and allowing your yielding action to provide you with the most natural deflection from all three frames. As you develop a sense of comfort and flow, see if you are able to move preemptively on occasion, before the push arrives, blending with the motion. The key is to look for the moment when time and distance permit preemptive movement. Don't become obsessed with avoiding contact or judging your movement. Just explore your responses, still allowing contact the majority of the time. You already know you can move with contact, so getting touched at this point is no big deal. Just play with the idea of occasionally injecting preemptive evasion when the time is right.

Option one: Your partner encroaches.

Preemptive evasion and middle-frame deflection.

Blending into a high frame and sticking to the strike.

Option two: same drill with low-framed deflection.

Kick loading.

Preemptive evasion and deflection.

Follow-up with reverse elbow.

EXERCISE 10
FOOTWORK

Have your partner hold a 3- to 4-foot-long stick and slowly begin swinging it at you. Remember that the stick more than doubles the length and speed of the arm, so even slow swings represent a considerable challenge. Treat the stick as if it were a sharp blade and being touched by it is not an option. Perform any manner of evasion you wish: ducking, jumping, stepping, or slipping. The goal of this phase of training is to maintain distance and give yourself as much reaction time as possible.

Your partner confronts you by swinging a stick at you.

You evade the downward swing.

Recover your balance.

Slip under his return.

Shield and come out the other side.

EXERCISE 11
THE JUNKYARD DOG DRILL

Have your partner stand with one heel touching the wall. His job will be to try to reach out and touch you at slow to medium speed. Your job is to start off outside his reach, at the same distance you were working during the previous stick drill. Your partner is not allowed to lose contact with the wall with his heel at any time.

Moving outside strike range.
(For the purpose of illustration, we used a medicine ball as the tether rather than a wall.)

ROUND 1: First, have your partner slowly swing at the air, trying to reach you at a distance where he cannot possibly touch you. Practice slipping and shielding against these "virtual" attacks, treating them as if they were in range. This is a

Slipping and rolling around the perimeter.

completely safe and comfortable way to explore your movement and build your natural reactivity.

ROUND 2: Slowly practice inching toward the attacker's range. As you approach the perimeter of his reach, practice evading and slipping his attempts. If the stress becomes too much, remember that just stepping back an inch or two will put you safely outside of his reach. Feel free to dip in and out as you need to endure the three rounds.

ROUND 3: Repeat Round 2, but now see if you are able to gently pat the incoming punches on occasion with the palm of your hands. These don't always need to touch. Sometimes, you will just twitch as if to reach and not actually make contact. Indulging the desire to reach without overextending will keep

Patting and checking the strike.

you moving and dynamic without necessarily sacrificing your balance or exposing you to hits. What matters most is that you are drilling a feeling of readiness. To quote Daniel Coyle, we want to get our nerves firing and failing so we know what to fix. You will find it much easier and quicker to pat with the inside of your palms rather than the outside of your hands (that's why you never see people on *Jeopardy* hitting their buttons with the backs of their hands). A helpful mantra is "insides of the palms for patting, outsides for shielding."

ROUND 4: Now see if you are able to go all the way into mid-range. As you move from the perimeter to mid-range, you need to move from patting to shielding. Pats, checks, and jab catches work but only at the outside range. Whenever people fail with these moves, they are invariably attempting them from too short a distance, where reaction time is reduced. Instead, turn your palms inward toward your head. Keep the hands high to protect the vulnerable backs of your hands from direct impacts and offer the spikes of your elbows instead. Remember to keep your shields in motion like you are washing your hair.

Working at midrange.

Shielding and driving inside close range.

EXERCISE 12
VISUALIZING DISTANCE

Close your eyes and take a deep breath. Imagine yourself standing in front of an aggressor who is a few steps away from you and safely out of hand-to-hand range but is screaming at you. You raise your open hands in front of your chest, palms outward toward the person, projecting passivity as you try to talk him down but improving your readiness.

The aggressor bolts forward while raising his hands and taunting you. He is just outside striking range but still looking for an opening, goading you to go first and make a mistake. You raise your hands slightly and begin shifting and circling slightly. Your hands are already moving naturally with casual gestures.

The attacker fires a tentative jab to probe the distance. You slip away and pat the jab while trying to calm him down. He darts forward, swinging a crazed barrage of hooks. You turn your palms inward and grab your head, emulating the action of washing your hair as you plunge safely beneath the blitz and drive forward to finish him off.

POINTS TO REMEMBER

- When you pat a long-range hit, you give your brain and body more information and help it map out a clearer understanding of where you and your opponent are in space.
- When you shield, turning the palms inward protects the vein and nerves of the more vulnerable inner forearms. It also functionalizes your flinch response: when you are surprised, your grasp reflex will make you instinctively reach forward to try and grab, which can damage the fingers and hands. By shielding, you turn your natural grasp reflex toward yourself, using it to protect your head rather than dangerously reaching for incoming force.

SECTION

2

The Russian martial arts are renowned for their striking power. Fluid, elliptical motions combined with a scientific understanding of structure, biomechanics, and breath integration result in an arsenal of unmatched power and fluidity. In the following section, we will address some of Combat Systema's most essential weapons.

BASIC STRIKING

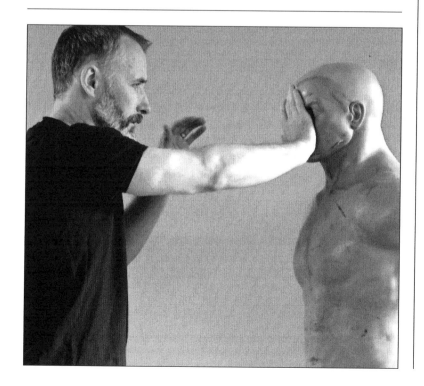

THE INSTANT STRIKE

Now that we have a basic understanding of long-, medium-, and close-range defense, we need to address our offensive capacities at each range. The long range is ideal for kicking and weapon use, but both of those take considerably more effort than what I am going to propose. In boxing, the basic perimeter shot would be a long jab. Even something as basic as a jab requires a lot of nuance and detail to be effective. A far simpler variation to learn is the finger whip.

Unlike many styles of martial arts that advocate a straight-line spearing action with the fingertips, the Combat Systema finger whip takes absolutely no conditioning. The fingers do not need to be tensed, bunched, or reinforced. Moreover, they do not need to be conditioned because they are not enduring any direct pressure. Instead, I simply reach out and tap my attacker in the eyes with the same finger pads I am using to type this instruction.

EXERCISE 13
THE FINGER WHIP

Stand with your elbow raised toward the side of your body at shoulder height. Keep the thumb of your open hand resting comfortably against your sternum and your palm facing the floor. Slowly elongate your arm out in front of your body, turning your thumb downward so that the pads of your fingers touch your intended target. It is a good idea to keep a small contraction in your elbow to avoid overextending it. Perform 10 slow repetitions, exhaling slowly as you extend.

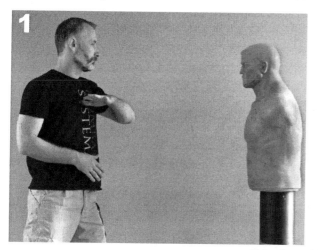

Side view of finger whip.

Front view of finger whip.

Next, perform 10 fast repetitions with a quick exhale on each one. Focus on bringing the hand back faster than you send it out. Working with the elbow raised in this manner will help you feel the speed of the strike and isolate the triceps.

Finally, lower your elbow to a more realistic defensive position with your palms in a more useful defensive position. Perform 10 reps toward your target.

TRAINING TIP: Hang a towel on a shower rod and practice striking it with your finger whip. Remember, the finger whip is a perimeter shot that you use when you are in long range, so generally your hands will be in a passive pre-engagement position. The goal of the finger whip is to temporarily shock and stun, so non-telegraphic delivery and speed are what matter. You don't even need to impact to trigger a flinch in your opponent.

Finger whip training on a towel.

DIRTY BOXING 101

Once you get inside striking range, you need to protect your head, moving your hands from a pre-engagement position into full shields. For this reason, you will need weapons that fire naturally from a shielded position. If you watch MMA, you will often see fighters using shields to protect against power punches but then generally retaliating with conventional boxing punches. This means they lose a beat by bringing their hand down from the top of their head, where they are shielding, to the cheek before throwing a punch. What we need is a shot that launches directly from the top of the head.

EXERCISE 14
THE LEAD HAMMERFIST

Begin in a shielded position with your palms touching the top of your head and your elbow jutting toward your opponent's face. Slowly close your lead hand into a fist as you elongate your arm. Contract harder and harder as you elongate until you arrive at your target. Remember to maintain a slight flexion in your elbow and freeze there a few seconds, contracting constantly to brand the muscle memory into your system. Return directly to your head. Perform 10 repetitions.

For your second set, deliver the hit at medium speed with medium contraction. Prac-

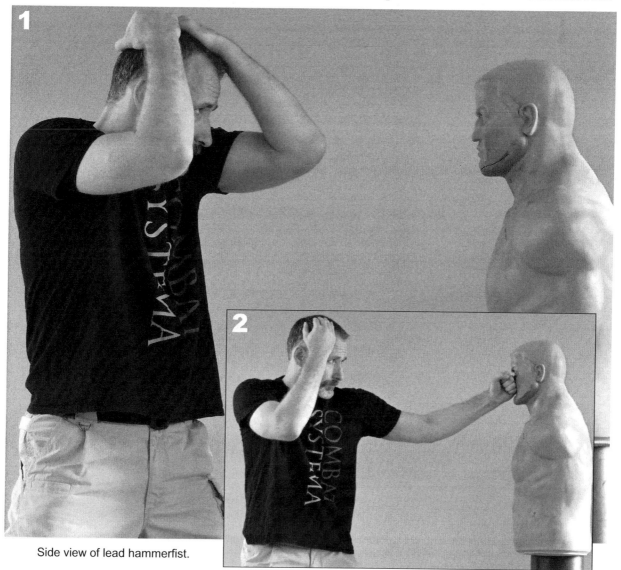

Side view of lead hammerfist.

tice sinking slightly as you deliver the hit, flexing at the knees to add power to the hit. It is ideal if you are able to hit an actual target, whether a focus mitt, punching bag, or your opponent's open hand. Perform 10 repetitions.

For your third set, evolve to a more fluid and powerful hit. After the point of impact, continue to drop your elbow until it reaches your body and then climb back up to the top of your head. Your hand will make a tight oval motion as if you were imitating the wheels on a train. This will generate a far more powerful, efficient, and fluid hammerfist that blends into other strikes effortlessly, as we will see shortly.

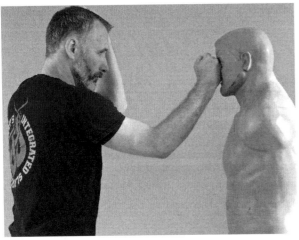

Hammerfist.

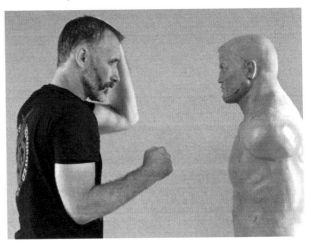

Follow-through.

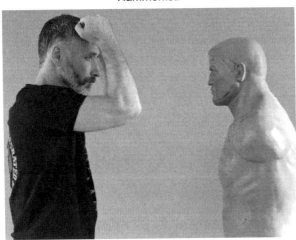

Return to stance.

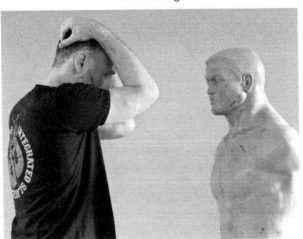

Shield.

STANCE DESTRUCTION

In the street, there is very little time to engage in a war of attrition with your opponent in order to gain access to targets like you might in sport fighting. One of the easiest ways to infiltrate your attacker's defensive stance is to destroy it. The hammerfist we used in the previous exercise works ideally against your opponent's face for a quick stun, but it can just as easily be used to smash his lead hand or forearm down to open the way for a follow-up strike to the face and trunk. Here are a few drills to give you some ideas.

EXERCISE 15
THE INFINITY STRIKE

Figure-eight motions play a huge role in many traditional Russian martial arts. They provide incredible power and flow, and open up huge variations for striking combinations. They are also liberating and healthier for your joints because they share load successively from one joint to another, unlike snapping, piston-like motions, which place more immediate pressure on a single joint.

OPTION 1: Return to the previous drill, dropping a downward hammerfist from your shielded position. This can be done with your lead hand as in Exercise 14 or your back hand as demonstrated in the photos. As your hand arrives at its lowest

Hammerfist.

Follow-through.

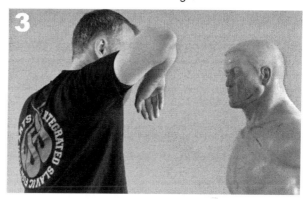
Load the elbow.

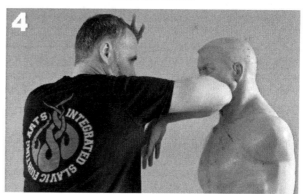
Cutting elbow.

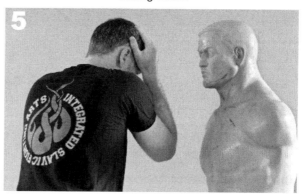
Return to shields.

point, begin raising your elbow so that it is higher than your hand and drop a diagonal cutting elbow into your opponent's face. After you have hit your target, circle your hand back up into a shielded motion, dropping your elbow back to your ribs. Practice this slowly. The goal is to work *within* the capacity of your joints. Keep the motion soft and small, and avoid repeated cracking in your joints or any stiff motions. We use the expression "round out the corners" to convey this goal. If you close your eyes and feel the motion, you will notice that it creates a slanted figure-eight form. These motions are often referred to as "infinity strikes" because not only does the motion look like you are tracing the infinity symbol, but it also does not need to end. You can chain figure-eight motions into a continuous flow of hits, as we will see shortly.

OPTION 2: Now begin with your hand on your opponent or striking target. Begin immediately with your lead elbow, rotating your elbow above your hand until it is on an angle, and cut downward on a diagonal into your target. After you have sliced through your target, think of returning with a downward hammerfist. In this variation, you have reversed the flow and shown how even the act of returning to your shields can be weaponized. For added power and emphasis, think of pivoting inward as you elbow and then return to your basic stance as you hammerfist back into stance. Notice again how your arm created a tight figure-eight motion.

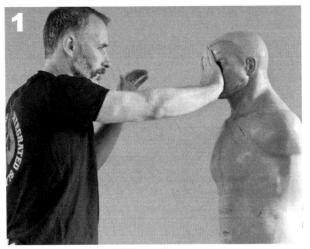
Palm on face.

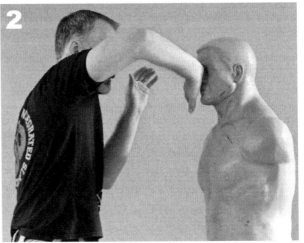
Load elbow.

Cutting elbow.

Follow-through.

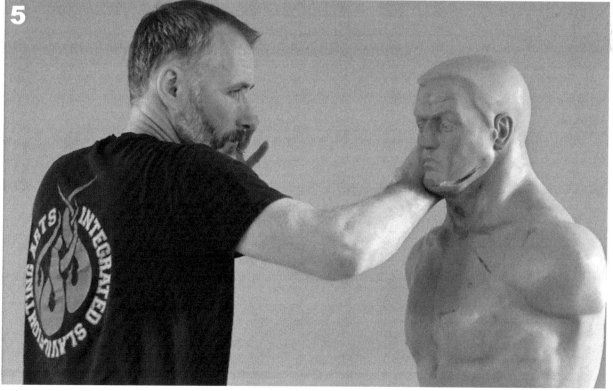

Return with hammerfist.

OPTION 3: Both drills used the same motion with different emphasis. Now, try putting them together so that you can hit three times in the same motion. Begin from a shielded position. Drop your lead hammerfist downward, raise and drop the elbow of the same arm in a diagonal cutting elbow, and then return to form with a final downward hammerfist. As you perform your three hits, your legs should sink, pivot, and return to stance, respectively.

Shield.

Lead hammerfist.

Follow-through.

Load the elbow.

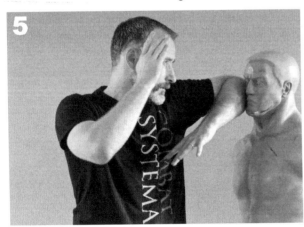

Cutting elbow.

Elbow follow-through.

Load the hammerfist.

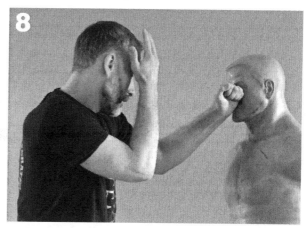

Hammerfist.

Return to shield.

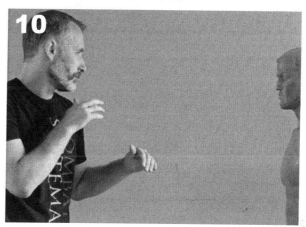

Clear.

EXERCISE 16
THE SLAVIC JAB

The figure-eight motion can be used in a huge variety of ways. One of the most typical that we find in the Russian martial arts is in what is termed "the Slavic jab." For simplicity's sake, we will build off the finger whip, introduced in Exercise 13, but you could just as easily build this from a fisted jab if you prefer.

Begin by firing off medium-speed finger whips. Remember to arrive with your thumb pointed downward so that you impact your target with the cushions of your hand. As you continue to train this, see if you can evolve the strike so that the retraction becomes slightly less linear. As your finger whip goes out, feel it drop slightly as it goes through the target and return slightly lower than it went out. The entire path will be like a very subtle, very compressed oval.

Finger whip.

Elliptical follow-through.

Load the hammerfist.

Hammerfist.

Return to stance.

Now, purely as an exploration, try firing off two consecutive finger whips on exactly the same path as quickly as possible. In time this will become quite comfortable, but initially most practitioners find this a little awkward if the motion is too linear.

Now, after firing your first finger whip, follow up with a hammerfist. What matters most here is that you vary the plane from which you are attacking. Notice, when you finger-whip, your thumb points down and your elbow is almost fully elongated and pointing up. When you ham-

merfist, your thumb is pointing up or to the side, depending on where you are hitting, and your elbow in considerably more bent and pointing down. Finger whips snap and push, and create distance. Hammerfists generally drop, drag, and rip, and create much more destructive strikes. If you perform your jab with a fist, the figure-eight feeling can be slightly larger since the initial hit is considerably heavier and more destructive, and the weight of the fist will tend to swing the forearm around the elbow like a propeller.

Stance.

Jab (as an option to the finger whip).

Elliptical follow-through.

Load.

Hammerfist.

In either form, the Slavic jab is a great way to fire the equivalent of a one-two combination using only your lead hand. The first shot stuns and baits, and then you follow up on a half or even a quarter beat before the attacker can adapt.

TRAINING TIP: Try practicing the motion very slowly with a small hand weight. Always perform the motion slowly when training with a weight to avoid damaging your joints. Move at a continuous pace and rhythm no matter how demanding to cultivate perfection in every aspect of your movement. Slow weight training lets you refine stance, pivot, transfer of weight, and breathing. Slow it down, and your improvements will speed up.

THE THREE ELBOWS

As we have seen, there are three fundamental frames that we use for deflections: the lower frame with the arms completely at our sides, the middle frame with our hands at chest level and our elbows winging up and down, and the upper frame when our hands are up on the head and shielding. As a result, there are three distinct types of elbow strikes that can be thrown: lower frame, middle frame, and upper frame.

EXERCISE 17
THE LOWER-FRAME ELBOW STRIKE

Begin with your arms hanging comfortably at your sides. From this position, the cupped palm of your hand will be touching the side of your thigh. To prepare the shoulder, practice slowly moving your elbow as far forward as you can, rolling your pinkie forward while maintaining thumb contact with your leg. Once the motion is comfortable, allow yourself to lose contact with your thigh and simply permit the elbow to whip forward through this same rotation. When striking with the lower-frame elbow, you impact with the outside meat of the elbow joint rather than the blade of the elbow. The lower-frame elbow is an extreme close-range strike that is used from a walking position to surprise and create distance.

To rotating arm forward with thumb as pivot on thigh.

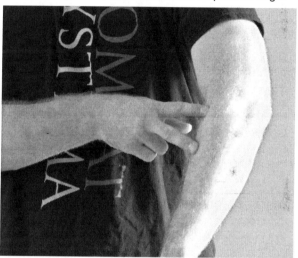
Striking surface.

Shoulder prep: rotating from palm facing thigh, then back, thumb on thigh.

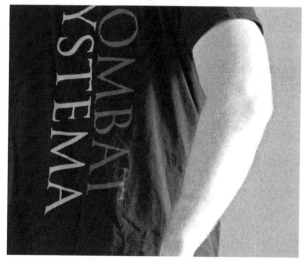
Striking surface without indication.

Load shoulder.

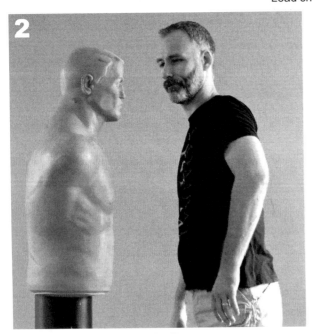

Launch elbow.

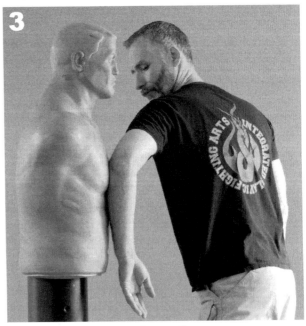

Lower-frame elbow.

EXERCISE 18
THE MIDDLE-FRAME ELBOW STRIKE

The second basic elbow strike is generally thrown from a middle frame. To learn the basic mechanics, however, it is easier to begin in a lower frame. With the arms hanging comfortably, raise your elbow directly up to the side of your body to shoulder height. You will notice it is far more comfortable to raise your elbow in line with the side of your body and that raising the elbow toward the front of your body strains the shoulder. As you practice, raise the elbow more and more quickly. You will notice that if you engage your biceps, snapping your hand up toward your chest and armpit, the elbow will rise far more quickly and arrive more solidly. We commonly refer to this as the "scarecrow position."

Once the elbow motion becomes comfortable, begin integrating a pivot. The most common error is to lean and reach for your target with the arm. The arm should only be responsible for raising the elbow, and distance should be generated from the legs pivoting. The impact surface should be the first few inches of the ulna.

This elbow is often referred to as a "quick elbow" because of the immediacy of the strike. It can be thrown from either a low or middle frame and is ideal for a quick stun and setup.

Lower-frame stance.

Middle-frame quick elbow.

Frontal view of middle-frame elbow strike.

EXERCISE 19
THE UPPER-FRAME ELBOW

Beginning in an upper frame, stretch your elbow up as high as you can reach, while allowing your hand to lower comfortably along your face. From this position, pivot cutting downward on a diagonal with your elbow. This elbow is often referred to as a "cutting elbow" because of the slicing nature of the hit. It is ideal for driving through stance and shields, and is an incredibly powerful strike capable of ending a fight in a single hit.

Upper frame.

Loading the elbow on a diagonal.

Cutting down with the elbow.

Option two from upper frame: straight upward elbow.

SECTION

3

Some of the most essential factors in combat are some of the most commonly overlooked. These include *proxemics,* the study of distance and space, and *kinesics,* the study of movement, touch, language, and paralanguage. In Combat Systema, we have six essential physical characteristics that we emphasize in our basics:

1. Blading
2. Zoning
3. Fencing
4. Loading the stance
5. Tactical vision
6. Tactical breathing

COMBAT ESSENTIALS

1. BLADING

The first consideration is the position of your body. During a crisis, the effects of stress can cause tunnel vision in an effort to focus your attention on the stress at hand. Sports optometrist Hal Breedlove showed that excitement of the sympathetic nervous system caused constriction of blood vessels in the retina, leading to up to a 70-percent reduction in peripheral vision. The simultaneous transfer to binocular vision will cause the body reflexively to square off with a threat. This can be seen in anyone who is being overwhelmed by intimidation. The individual will tend to leave his body flush with his aggressor and often cause the victim to stumble back nervously on his heels. This is caused by tunnel vision. It's as if the subject is looking at the world through a cheap camera, which forces him to back up in order to get a better view.

The first preventive measure we can take is to consciously turn our body to a slight angle when we sense danger. If you think of your body like the blade of the knife, you want to decrease the exposure of the flat of your body and increasingly turn the edge of your side to the opponent. You are looking for 30 to 45 degrees of rotation. Anything more can needlessly expose your vulnerable back. It should be remembered that this will not override your body's reflexes, but it can go a long way to delay their onset by keeping you in a tactically superior position that helps increase awareness.

Blading the body also places the vulnerable targets located along the body's centerline on a natural deflection path. When you are standing flush and are sucker punched, you take the bulk of the impact and stumble back, remaining in the line of fire. When you are bladed, your body is more likely to twist and squat, helping to deflect the force. Blading also helps you better define your personal space by jutting your lead shoulder forward and gives you more distance and time for your rear hand to respond, whether it be by drawing a weapon, shielding, or counterstriking.

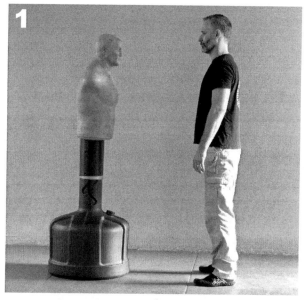

Start square to partner.

Bladed stance.

EXERCISE 20
BLADING

Begin by simply having a partner stand in front of you at a comfortable distance. It is best if both of you keep your bodies square to one another. Next, have your partner take one step forward and wait. Notice if you feel any changes in your body. Repeat this exercise one step at a time, always taking time at each interval to notice if there is any change.

At some point, regardless of how familiar you are with your partner, you will likely notice a feeling of increased awareness or even discomfort. When this happens, take your time to feel what is occurring. Is your breathing accelerating? Can you feel a difference in your pulse? Can you feel tension arising in areas of your body?

Now try blading your body. When you have a choice, it is preferable to keep your strong side back. If you are right-handed, step back on the right side. This will serve you in accessing a weapon and also readies your strong side for power strikes.

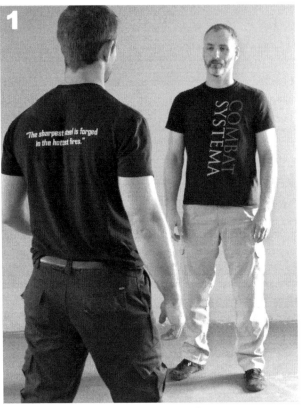

Second perspective: squared to partner.

Starting position.

Second perspective: bladed to partner.

Bladed.

2. ZONING

The next consideration is the distance of your body from your opponent. As we have seen, the tendency in a crisis is to square with your opponent. Another tip for helping to maintain reaction time is to try to avoid standing directly in front of your aggressor. In boxing, fighters learn how to circle to the outside of their opponent's lead hand in order to increase the distance between themselves and their attacker's power hand. They then learn how to break this rhythm by circling inward to set up their own combinations. In exactly the same way, we seek to begin by positioning ourselves to the outside of an opponent's lead hand. This will increase your reaction time to power shots and help you see his actions more clearly.

EXERCISE 21
ZONING

Repeat the previous exercise. This time, instead of having your partner stop after each step, have him slowly and continuously saunter inward without emotion. The moment you feel uncomfortable, practice taking a step back and at an angle with your rear foot. This will allow you to both blade and zone in one simple and natural action.

Zoned.

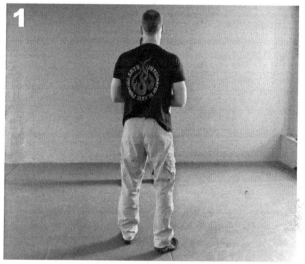

View from the rear: bladed.

Bladed and zoned.

View from the rear: bladed and zoned.

If you try making the movement too obvious, your aggressor may notice. This can trigger aggression and escalation, and cause him to react. A good way to keep the movement natural is to imagine the position of your chin, as if an imaginary line were running down through the center of it to the ground. Simply step aside so that you replace your chin on that line with your lead shoulder. When this is combined with blading, the action becomes very subtle and dramatically increases your defensive potential.

3. FENCING

The next step is to functionalize your hands, which is essential for both protecting you and enabling effective counterattacks. A common error is to keep your arms stiffly by your sides as your aggressor encroaches on you. Many people mistakenly confuse a lack of response with acting casual. They think that by not acknowledging the threat, they will appear more confident, or that raising their hands will somehow incite aggression. The reality is that if your aggressor is trying to gauge your defensive capacities and you fail to acknowledge him, he will continue to perceive you as a victim.

You absolutely want to bring your hands up whenever possible. This will immediately put space between you and your aggressor and help increase your reaction time. This also brings your tools closer to your aggressor's vital targets and allows you to shield your face more quickly. The key is to keep your actions natural and justified by context. Keep your hands open to project passivity. This will also serve you legally if you are forced to justify your actions in court by reinforcing your effort to remain nonviolent. It is beneficial strategically in that it allows you to infiltrate an aggressor's defenses and strike him with less warning than if you had closed your fists and expressed your intent or willingness. Pragmatically, it also helps discourage the fight from occurring by showing that you are alert.

Remember that anyone who attacks you because you passively raised your hands and stepped back was likely intending to attack any-

way. You did not trigger his actions. United Kingdom self-defense guru Geoff Thompson coined the term "fence" for this type of posture, and I will use his language here.

EXERCISE 22
THE FENCE

Have your partner repeat the same drill. But this time, blade, zone, and practice bringing your hands up in a natural and comfortable fence. Here are some options:

- The most common option is to simply keep your elbows tightly against your body and your hands open and at chest level.
- In less excited circumstances, you may feel

High-profile fence with your hands open.

more comfortable keeping your hands to-gether in front of your chest or, at greater distances, in front of your belt. Avoid inter-locking your fingers because involuntary contractions when startled can tie you up. Simply place one hand on top of the other.

• In some encounters, crossing the arms may feel more comfortable. As with interlocking your fingers in the previous example, you should avoid grapevining your arms to-gether. Simply fold your arms on top of each other.

High-profile fence with your hands clasped in front.

High-profile fence with your arms folded together.

EXERCISE 23
PREEMPTIVE STRIKING

Have your partner stand in front of you, holding a focus mitt. Begin in any preferred defense position, blading, zoning, and fencing. Focus purely on speed, delivering the fastest finger whip you can from your chosen starting position. You will notice that once you prioritize speed, the tendency is to freeze in your stance beforehand, making your intentions evident. Instead, try to keep your fence fluid and natural, moving in small gestures, pointing, scratching your head, cupping your hands together and then separating them, so that you are able to hide your intent and launch your finger whip from any position.

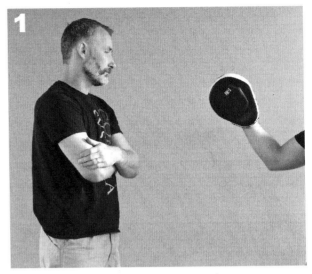

Start with arms crossed.

Use conversation . . .

. . . or point to distract.

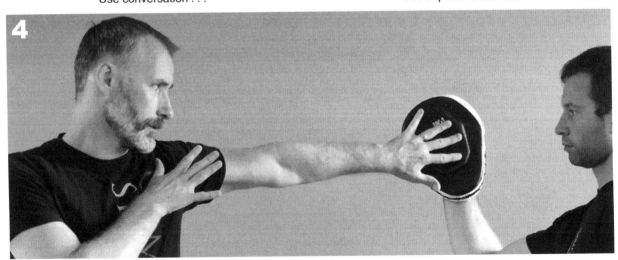

Finger whip.

EXERCISE 24
SPEED SHIELDING

Another simple yet important drill is to practice shielding against a sucker punch. Begin in your passive stance (bladed and zoned out), with your hands up and open and facing your aggressor. When you shield, you must turn your hands inward and grab the top of your head as quickly as possible. As simple as this action is, it can never be refined enough. When you are trying to defuse a situation and an aggressor tries to sucker punch you, there is no room for doubt or lack of confidence. Train this in the air, while facing a mirror, or with a partner throwing a sudden strike to make the action second nature.

Trying to verbally defuse a situation.

Using a speed shield against a sucker punch.

EXERCISE 25
RESOLVING MULTIPLE ATTACKERS

Have two training partners stand in front of you. A common tendency is for people to become preoccupied with a single attacker. In zoning against an attacker on the left, they can become more vulnerable to the aggressor on the right. The feeling of getting funneled increases, and there is a greater tendency to back up in a straight line. It is essential that you always seek to zone the group. Imagine a line extending from the centerline of each of the aggressors and converging on you. You always want to step to the outside of this junction. For this initial stage of training, it is enough to simply create the reflex of moving and improving your position.

In the case of three or four attackers, you will usually have someone behind you or trying to get there. In these cases, as you zone to one side, turn your head slightly so that you are able to glimpse behind you without losing sight of your frontal aggressors in your peripheral vision. This progression from one, two, and additional aggressors must be trained continuously until it becomes natural and instinctive. Too often, people notice that a second or third aggressor is moving in behind them, but they ignore the threat and allow it to happen. Simply knowing that someone is behind you is not enough. You must maintain sight of him whenever possible, and I strongly advise integrating verbal commands.

You are between two aggressors.

Zone away from the collective.

VERBAL DE-ESCALATION

Verbal skills are one of the most neglected aspects of combative training. I was very verbal most of my life: school president, valedictorian, writing novels at 16. When I was a young adult, I worked as a doorman to pay rent and got into telemarketing by day to be able to eat. I excelled in that world and quickly became a trainer, evolving into all manner of corporate training. There was a period of my life where I was a sponge, soaking up every type of sales training you could find, from Zig Ziglar to Anthony Robbins, and studying hypnosis, Neuro-Linguistic Programming, and even stage magic. For a good part of those early years, I was still working the door at clubs on weekends. That was a pivotal moment for me, because I got to see just how far you could push the power of words to reduce aggression. There is a lot more at stake when the angry customer has a knife in his hand. So I recognized that I had a very rare and fortunate series of circumstances to awaken my motivation.

Most people don't understand how important verbal skills are. No matter how well I teach them, there are always a few students who are looking at the floor and yawning within the first minute. A good portion of the world just wants to learn cool moves and go full ninja when faced with aggression—at least in their fantasies. I wish I could give you some incredible trick for awakening these types to the need, but I have yet to find one. I can only say, if you are an instructor, keep exposing your students to the importance of verbal skills. If you yourself have already considered flipping ahead to our section on "cosmic death touches of the black arts," I promise I will keep the verbal work short so that everyone can walk out with some simple ideas that have saved my life. Here are just a few simple exercises.

EXERCISE 26
BREATH CONTROL UNDER STRESS

Your emotional state will affect your ability to employ meaningful commands enormously. Research at Minnesota State University showed that law enforcement officers who felt over-whelmed or deeply threatened generally lost the capacity to communicate effectively. Some would argue that this is proof that verbal skills are limited to ideal situations and can't work when it matters. I would say first that this research rather reinforces the massive importance of blading, zoning, fencing, and maintaining distance and situational awareness to offset that type of panic and prolong your verbal threshold. I would also say that you will fight how you train. If you pay verbal skills only lip service (pun intended), they will not magically appear under stress. I have trained them in myself, as well as in many professionals, and they have been there when we needed them most.

TRAINING TIP: People generally don't know where to start when they want to incorporate verbal skills. Scenario training can be very awkward at first. People giggle, get quiet, overdo it and get insulting, or otherwise turn it into a joke. To side-step this discomfort, start by just having students talk through physically demanding drills:

• Have students jog side by side or wrestle or box with the objective of maintaining a fluid conversation on any topic.

Practice talking while wrestling.

- Drop and perform a set of push-ups until you are exhausted with reduced or restricted breathing and then stand up and practice recovering your breath as you talk. This is the exact same skill you will need to stay verbal under stress. The key is to speak in small seg-

ments, filling in the gaps with eye contact and gestures to probe for attention. This will help you get your breath back without looking like you're winded. Just a little bit of regular practice will make this familiar and also massively increase your ability to recover from panic.

Practice your breathing exercises while performing a push-up.

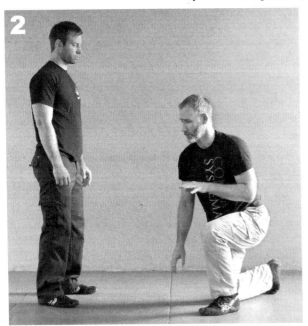

Stand up.

Regain your breath while talking.

EXERCISE 27
ASSESSING YOUR RESPECTFULNESS

Research has shown that subjects who feel respected are more likely to comply. Write down some of the phrases you would use to de-escalate an aggressor and then take a look at the language. Are there any words in there that might be perceived as condescending? Obviously, you need to get rid of any slurs, denigrating terms, or demeaning implications. Even innocent terms like "buddy" should be replaced by "sir." Keep things respectful.

Also keep things simple and clear. Ambiguous language can get you killed. Phrases like "stop that," "move," and "relax" may be well intended, but they lack clarity. Stop what? Move where? Relax how? Be specific:

- "I need you to take your hands out of your pocket right now, sir."
- "Please take two steps back. Take two steps back, please."
- "Please stay seated in your chair."
- "Drop the knife now. Drop the knife!"

"I need you to take your hands out of your pocket right now, sir."

Getting back to our earlier example of multiple attackers, I have generally needed to use phrases like: "All right, that's far enough, guys. I'm going to have to ask you to take a step back." If the context is more intense, it might be something as simple as repeating a command: "Stop! Stop! Please sit back down!"

I have had situations where things were friendly enough but it was apparent the subjects were trying to circle me. I immediately became serious and pointed at the individual encroaching my rear flank and said, "You need to stop right there. Stay where I can see you," while engaging in a few seconds of confident eye contact. Then I returned to defusing the first aggressor, in a newly zoned position that allowed me to keep the second subject in my peripheral vision. Context will dictate what is appropriate, but know that it is a good idea to acknowledge and engage people who think they are getting away with something unseen.

CRACKING

Certain rituals often precede a conflict. The so-called "interview" phase can allow an aggressor the ability to assess your vulnerabilities and determine whether and how he wishes to retaliate. In the case of ambushes, the interview stage can consist entirely of being observed remotely. In other instances, it can include face-to-face escalation, including questions, threats, and taunts. In the case of multiple attackers, aggressors may not always begin or remain at a distance. They can press directly into your personal space and smother your defensive capacities. In these situations, it is necessary to slip, push, or break your way out of the mob. This is what we refer to as "cracking" the mob. Under no circumstances should you feel content to remain centered in a group of aggressors.

When three or more individuals are directly pressed up against you, you will lack the space to feel any significant difference from zoning or blading. Still, you should try to drive your lead shoulder into the closest aggressor. It is helpful to raise your lead shoulder as well and to tuck your chin to protect your neck from sucker punches. This subtle shift will allow you to jut your hips back slightly and to raise your hands to at least a middle frame. Your arms can help create wedges and frames to make space and enable you to slip out of the group.

EXERCISE 28
THE BUS DRILL

There is an excellent drill to help develop an intuitive understanding of this feeling. Have two or more partners stand side by side. They may begin simply by having their shoulders tightly pressed together and then can evolve to wrapping their arms around their necks or backs. They may even overlap their legs. The goal is to practice slipping between partners. The key is to lead with your hand or foot and to snake and spiral the limbs through to create a wedge. When passing the head through, tuck it deeply into your shoulder. After making it through with your body, turn toward your partners to facilitate pulling your trailing limbs out.

This simple drill teaches you essential principles about breaking through a tight wall of people. When you return to combative drills, you will generally find the spaces between them larger and getting through easier. As comfort increases, the partners can don gloves and begin punching and striking to add interference. When practicing this, protect your head at all times. "Washing your hair" with high shields is highly effective and will allow you to push and spike with your elbows. Avoid competing with the group and striking back as this will generally open you up to getting hit. Stay shielded, step, and push in all directions with your elbows as you shield to create distance until you find an exit from the group. Once you have cracked the mob, turn to address the group, zoning out immediately to line them up as close to single file as possible rather than allowing them to attack as a wall.

1

Begin behind a wall of students.

2

Wedge in with your leg.

3

Follow with your arm.

4

Twist to pull through.

5

Come out the other side.

6

Arrive in your stance.

4. LOADING THE STANCE

A fourth essential aspect of a high-probability survival posture is to *load* your stance. Reflex, as we have seen, will often turn us square to our opponent because of our binocular tunnel vision. This can also cause you to lean back with the head, sacrificing balance, and ultimately to turn the head and waist away, offering up your back to attack. It is commonly said that regular people run away from danger while heroes run toward it. This reflex to run away begins at a most primal biological level. One simple trick for increasing the probability that you will be able to move toward an attack is to simply keep your rear heel lifted. This will immediately increase the probability that you will duck, flexing in the knees to better evade and absorb impact, rather than turning away and giving your back. With training, it will also lend itself to moving forward, inside the power line of incoming strikes.

EXERCISE 29
RUNNING TOWARD DANGER

Here are a few drills to help reinforce the importance of a loaded stance:

- Place a strap or sturdy belt around your waist. Have a partner hang off it like he is water skiing, firmly planting his feet on the ground. Make every effort to move forward and drag your partner, regardless of whether you are able to advance. This will go a long way toward reinforcing correct alignment and the importance of driving off the balls of your feet.

- Have a partner piggyback on you. Begin in a resting stance with your feet shoulder-width apart, keep your tailbone engaged at all times (as seen in Exercise 4), and practice entering into your loaded stance. To remain consistent, think of blading, zoning, and fencing as you do so. Then return to your resting stance and repeat.

- Beginning with just your body weight, practice loading your basic stance. You will notice that when your rear heel is up and you are driving lightly off the ball of your foot more weight will be on your lead foot. In this position, it will be impossible to raise your lead foot and keep it off the ground without leaning back and putting your rear heel back on the ground. Practice trying to lift your lead foot off the ground and fall forward onto the lead foot. This type of quick lunging action is an immediate way to measure and gain strength and balance in your legs. As your comfort level grows, you can repeat this exercise while carrying a partner on your back.

Belt drag.

Piggyback.

Practice loading your basic stance.

KINESICS

With very little practice, you will begin to integrate blading, zoning, fencing, and loading intuitively. The most essential aspect of these four postural considerations is that they blend together in a natural and justifiable series of actions. They should never be static and frozen. Instead, they should be a casual blur of everyday motions.

We are all experts on body language (kinesics). We interpret facial expressions and gestures every day, in all that we do, without conscious thought. Moreover, we are primed as individuals to look for meaning in these actions. In learning to improve our defenses, we need to study the role that incorporating natural motion can play in concealing our intent. We should strive to become nothing less than masters of motion.

EXERCISE 30
STRIKING FROM MOTION

Begin in front of a striking target. Start in a comfortable stance, bladed, zoned, fenced, and loaded. Have a conversation, moving your hands in a natural manner. As you move your hands, practice launching the finger whip from your gestures. You will quickly see there are some actions with which you are more comfortable. Here are a few examples:

- Gesture comfortably, defining your space with your hands. In the middle of your conversation, refer to something in the distance and point to a spot behind your aggressor. If he turns to look, launch your finger whip to his eyes immediately. If he does not look, look at the spot you are pointing to for an instant, maintaining your focus on the aggressor in your peripheral vision and immediately launch your finger whip.

Defusing a situation.

Pointing to distract: aggressor looks back.

While your aggressor is distracted
by your pointing, employ a finger whip.

- As you are gesturing, point to a spot on his stomach, look down for a second, and then launch your finger whip immediately. You will find it easiest to reach slightly across your body with the back of your hand slightly toward your aggressor to best set up the finger whip.
- In the case of two or more aggressors, practice gesturing back and forth between them. For example, you might say: "Doesn't one of you own that car?" as you point back and forth between them a few times to distract them. The idea is just to get your hand bouncing back and forth between them, in order to get them used to your moving quickly. You might even get them look-ing behind themselves. If they are antic-ipating any fast motion from you, the gesture will trigger a sudden retreat or flinch, in effect helping you gauge their readiness and making them waste their reflexive action. If they do not react or if their awareness subsides during the gesture, they will have in effect lowered their guard.

TRAINING TIP: Blading, zoning, fencing, and loading should be practiced constantly in your daily life. With very little practice, they will become second nature. Integrate them in the way you stand on the bus, walk through a crowd, converse with colleagues, and conduct other everyday actions.

Begin by trying to discuss the situation.

Point to his stomach.

3

When he looks down at his stomach, employ a finger whip.

5. TACTICAL VISION

"You will come to be able to actually beat men in fights, and to be able to win with your eyes."

—Miyamoto Musashi
The Book of Five Rings

The fifth consideration is the use of the eyes. While it has already been mentioned that tunnel vision can significantly affect our behavior in a crisis, an additional consideration is the role of influence. People instinctively use eye contact to intimidate. Journalist William Nack joked that boxing champion Sonny Liston was so intimidating that his opponents would start to bleed during the national anthem when he glared at them across the ring. People also naturally avert their eyes when they are trying to hide something. Remember how when you forgot to do your homework, the very last thing you wanted to do was look at the teacher—ironically, that's always probably why she knew to pick you. Beyond determining how much information we gather, how we use our eyes will largely determine whether we are perceived as a victim or a fellow predator. So, the eyes are a big part of escalation or diffusion in a conflict.

The good news is that vision can be trained.

EXERCISE 31
DEVELOPING A STARE

The last thing we want to do is stare at an opponent, but in order to use our eyes efficiently we need to be in control of them. A good first step is to practice your stare in a mirror. Even making eye contact with yourself will train your eye muscles and get you used to the physiological changes this can trigger in your body.

While staring in the mirror, practice slowly raising your chin an inch while maintaining a focal point. Hold this for a few breaths and then return to center. Now practice lowering your chin an inch lower than normal and hold for a few breaths. You will notice that when you raise your chin, there is no change in your visual field. In fact, your eyes can sometimes feel like they widen. When you lower your chin, you will likely begin to see your brow slightly in your peripheral vision. This narrowing of vision mildly replicates the effect of tunnel vision, which is intended to assist your focus. It can go a long way toward keeping your eyes relaxed and confident.

My eyes have always been prone to fatigue. After a long night of working the door at a club, with flashing lights and smoke filling the air (remember, kids, people used to be allowed to smoke in clubs), my eyes would be sore and blinky. I quickly learned that in a conflict, if I consciously tried to squint my eyes while keeping my chin high, they still felt tired. If I simply lowered my chin, however, they relaxed more and I felt more confident and was perceived that way.

One ex-Spetsnaz operative with whom I trained said it was helpful to think only of what you would be willing to do to an attacker. He cautioned: "Do not think of killing the individual if you would only be willing to break his finger. Instead of thinking about breaking his finger in the fullest detail, fill your mind only with this as you talk to him and he will see it in your eyes."

EXERCISE 32
LOW-LIGHT TRAINING

Another interesting variation of the mirror drill is to perform the exercise in candlelight. The low light combined with the erratic flickering of the candle allows you to relax much more deeply, so you can pursue the training for much longer periods. A combination of the play of shadows and the deeper relaxation can play tricks on the mind and allow deeper fears and thoughts to emerge in your thoughts. Think of this as a very simple meditation with direct combat applications. It suffices to perform this on occasion. You may be surprised at what thoughts arise during this exercise.

A key to being effective in extreme low light is to not look at the light source. In nature, this means avoiding eye contact with the moon. In this exercise it means never staring at the candle directly. You will be amazed how powerfully your eyes can adjust to the dark.

EXERCISE 33
REHABILITATING THE EYES

After these exercises, or any stressful event, it is helpful to allow the eyes to rest. One great drill is to simply close your eyes. This immediately frees the optical lenses from any need to focus. Keeping the eyes closed, practice slowly moving them in the fullest possible circles. Move 10 times clockwise and then 10 times counterclockwise. With the eyes still closed, move them up to one corner and then down to the opposite corner 10 times and then switch the angle. Finally look slowly up and then down 10 times and then side to side 10 times. This simple drill helps massage the lenses and leaves the eyes relaxed, refreshed, and strengthened.

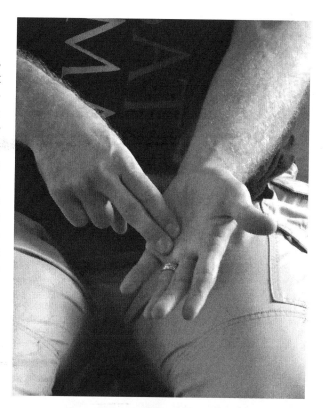

Closed-eye drill.

Another great exercise is to close your eyes and rub the palm of your hands together vigorously for 20 seconds. Then, press your palms or fingers onto your closed eyes. The heat will immediately soothe the eyes. This can be repeated a few times. Remember to thoroughly wash your hands before doing this exercise.

Rub your fingertips together to warm them and then rub your eyelids with them to soothe the eyes.

EXERCISE 34
IDENTIFICATION DRILLS

Here is another great drill that we use for eye speed. Create two sheets of paper: one with the letters A through Z randomly scattered on it, and the second with the numbers 1 through 26 jumbled across it. For an extra challenge you can vary the font size. Stick the sheets side by side and stand roughly 6 feet in front of them. Without moving your head, practice first finding the numbers in order and then the letters. Then for an added challenge, pair them (e.g., 1-a, 2-b, 3-c). This is a great scanning drill that increases eye speed and processing time very quickly. For added challenges, add a stressor, such as performing a set of push-ups, while scanning.

H	M	C	Z	Q	6	2	26	13	5
W	G	A	I	P	10	19	8	11	
K	E	R	N	O	17	9	12	4	14
J	U	B	S	X J	23	16	22	18	
V	F	T	Y	D	1	20	3	7	24
					15	25	21		

Identifying a random assortment of letters and numbers can improve your eye speed.

EXERCISE 35
THE SLIDE STEP

Our eyes are tightly connected to our intentions. When we hear or sense something behind us, we instinctively turn to see what it is. As a doorman, I have seen aggressors tap someone on the shoulder from behind or call that person's name and then sucker punch him in the moment of vulnerability when he is turning. A good habit to drill is to have someone tap, push, or call you from behind. Rather than turning directly on the spot, take a single step forward with your preferred power leg on an angle, and raise your hands as you turn so that you arrive bladed, zoned, fenced, and loaded. For example, if you are right-handed, step on a slight diagonal toward your left, plant the ball of your right foot, and pivot to your left. Someone pushing or calling you from behind is usually expecting you to just turn on the spot. By simply moving away and at an angle, you interrupt his train of thought and usually earn a delay. You also arrive in a solid and familiar position rather than risking a hit on a narrow, twisted base.

When you feel a shoulder tap . . .

. . . if you turn incorrectly on the spot, you get hit . . .

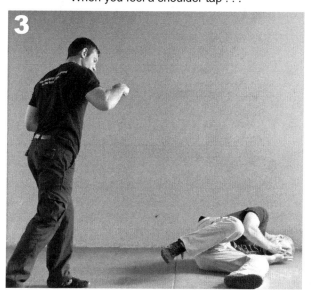

. . . and could end up knocked out.

Shoulder tap.

Slide step away.

By stepping away, you increase the odds of avoiding a strike and can assume a solid stance to counterattack.

EXERCISE 36
THREAT DETECTION

Have two partners stand side by side, 6 feet or more away from you. Turn your back to them. Have one of them draw a training knife and place it anywhere—it can be partially under a foot, visibly tucked in a belt, in the hand, balanced on a shoulder, or under an armpit. On their signal, take a step forward and then turn around like we did in the previous exercise. Try to spot the knife as quickly as possible and call out its location. The idea here is to break any expectations you might have about where the weapon "should" be and teach yourself to see, rather than just look.

Begin with your back turned to your partners.

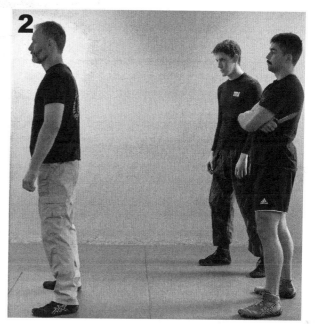

One of the partners places a knife in an obscured or unorthodox position.

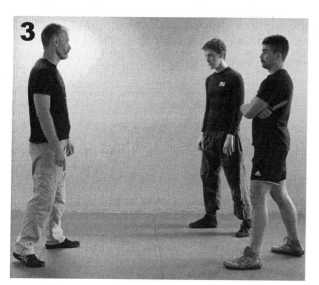

Slide step away, turn and scan the situation.

The first priority is to identify the location of the weapon.

EXERCISE 37
EYE CONTACT

Another aspect of maintaining control of your eyes is to avoid fixating on a single focal point. The challenge is that you still must engage in eye contact with your aggressor. Avoiding eye contact can be perceived as a lack of respect or a sign of submission, and both of those can trigger—you guessed it—more aggression. Likewise, excessive eye contact can be perceived as challenging or defiant. As a general rule, practice engaging in 1–2 seconds of eye contact every three.

Imagine that a large and intimidating aggressor is standing in front of you. He is visibly angry and staring directly at you. You can feel his eyes burning a hole through you. You acknowledge the individual with eye contact as you begin interacting with him. You can feel the weight of his stare. Your breath and pulse begin to race. You look away for an instant to his throat and then come back to his eyes. The switch helps you stay in control. You can feel your brain staying engaged with this goal. When you look away to his shoulder, you nod and continue to show that you are listening, always maintaining a clear awareness of the person in your peripheral vision.

One tactic that I have used dozens of times is to look slightly over an aggressor's shoulder and shake my head slightly, as if I were signaling back that I did not yet require assistance. On only one occasion did an aggressor ignore my "suggestion." At a minimum, the individuals' eyes would scan nervously to where I was glancing. In most cases, they would turn their head to some degree and de-escalate for a period out of concern. When I trained agents for the Montreal international airport, one tactic the team had great success with was to look up at the nearest security camera during an escalation. Subjects would often ask: "What's that?" to which the agents would respond, "It's a security camera. There are more than 300 of them in this area," and they would continue talking. Often, that was enough to get things back to a more civil tone.

Make eye contact for one to two seconds.

Look at the throat to regain control and then return to eye contact.

Option two: Look over the aggressor's shoulder.

6. TACTICAL BREATHING

The sixth physical essential that we seek to incorporate in our regular movement and gesture is effective breathing. Breathing is unique among body functions. Along with blinking, it is one of only two body functions that can be either autonomic (involuntary) or conscious (limited only by the breaking point of breath holding at one extreme or the loss of consciousness by hyperventilation at the opposite extreme). Unlike blinking, breathing allows us to indirectly control other autonomic functions of our body, including our pulse, emotions, degree of relaxation, and focus. Throughout the history of religious, spiritual and martial traditions, breathing has long been recognized as a key component of both health and combat functionality.

Research has shown conclusively that breathing behavior can be modified. We are not condemned to be bad breathers. In fact, our growing understanding of how to control our breathing patterns has earned breath retraining an increasingly central role as a fundamental component of psychological treatment. Breath retraining has been shown to improve lung disease, panic attacks, stress-induced psychosomatic complaints (e.g., carpal-tunnel syndrome) and chronic fatigue syndrome.[1]

During a crisis, our body reflexively causes us to hold our breath. Breath holding is an adaptive response that helped our ancestors hide better and to swim both to flee and hunt under water.[2] When we hold our breath, our abdominal muscles compress our gut, restricting the movement of our diaphragm. This transfers the demand for expansion to the intercostal muscles.[3]

There are two fundamental causes of breath-holding:

• The first is the startle response, which is triggered by sudden, intense stimuli. It includes a spasmodic, gasping inhale followed by a stop (apneusis).
• The second is the orientation response, which is triggered by the body's attempt to find the source of a stimulus (i.e., "What is that?"). It is characterized by a complete halt to breathing (apnea). You effectively forget to breathe entirely.

A shortness of breath (dyspnea) can also occur through a loss of voluntary control, like when we get the wind knocked out of us during training. In addition, secondary breath holds, like panic attacks, can be triggered by anticipation in individuals who have this conditioned response.[4]

For others, stress can have the opposite effect and trigger hyperventilation. This is an adaptive response intended to take in more air than your body needs to prepare it for fighting or fleeing a threat.[5] Typically, this induces a degree of panic, wherein individuals instinctively try to compensate by inhaling through the mouth (because it is larger) to satisfy the sensation of breath deprivation. Overbreathing is likely a factor in producing the symptoms of panic but it is not a direct cause. This means that overbreathing is *not* a physiological trigger, but rather a psychophysical one that affects only some individuals. This means it can be treated by either physically retraining breath patterns or by psychologically reframing and restructuring perception and expectations of the symptoms. Tightly connected to this, the process of

1. Ley, R., "The Modification of Breathing Behavior: Pavlovian and Operant Control in Emotion and Cognition," *Behavior Modification*, Vol.23., No. 3 (July 1999): 441–479.
2. Ibid.
3. Lang, P.B., "Emotion, Attention, and the Startle Flinch Reflex," *Psychological Review*, 97 (1990): 337–398.
4. Aitken, R.Z., "Some Psychological and Phsyiological Considerations of Breathlessness," In R.P. (Ed.), Breathing: Hering-breuer Centenary Symposium. London: Churchill (1970).
5. Ley, "Modification of Breathing Behavior," 441–479.

breath retraining provides a cognitive distraction from emotional processes and diverts the subject from focusing on anxiety.[6]

The first principle of tactical breathing is to breathe in through the nose and out through the mouth. We breathe in through the nose to combat the tendency to over-breathe and out through the mouth to maximize expulsion. It should be noted that tactical breathing differs from relaxation breathing, wherein an individual may breathe far more slowly and entirely by the nose.

Most people regard breathing as consisting of two phases (the inhale and the exhale). In reality, there are actually four sections that are each worthy of equal attention and training:

- Inhale
- Fullness
- Exhale
- Emptiness

During periods of rest, healthy individuals experience a slight natural pause between the inhalation and the exhalation, and the exhalation and the inhalation. Like a pendulum, the breath pauses briefly at each extreme. You can observe this while you are resting or see it in others who are in a comfortable and stress-free state. Cycling the breath faster and rushing through these natural pauses (or eliminating them completely) creates more stress in the body and cannot be maintained for great periods without harming your health. Mindful cultivation of these pauses, what we term *controlled pauses,* helps bring awareness to your breathing and can bring the body down from states of extreme arousal. These pauses permit a fuller processing of the breath and help avoid the risk of overbreathing, along with the tension and increased pulse rate, loss of cognitive control, and loss of motor function, which so often accompany this excitation.

In military and law enforcement circles, this four-cycle breath is often referred to as *tactical breathing.* The use of exaggerated pauses allows the practitioner to reduce the total number of breaths taken (decreasing breath *rate*) and increasing the *depth* of the breaths taken. The rate and depth are the two keys to avoiding overbreathing. A good part of the success of the square or tactical breathing method is the simple measurement it provides. Any time we feel ourselves accelerated, by reverting to a square breath, we can immediately measure what aspect of our breath needs to be adjusted. As a placebo mechanism, breath retraining allows us to decrease activity in pain-sensitive areas of our brain, assisting in the release of natural opioid mechanisms, and increasing activity in our prefrontal cortex, distracting us from emotion and pain.[7, 8] Numerous studies have clearly shown that voluntary changes in breathing patterns can positively affect an individual's capacity to cope with pain and their ability to manage deep fear and anxiety.[9]

6.   Garssen, B., "Clinical Aspects and Treatment of the Hyperventilation Syndrome," *Behavioral Psychotherapy* 14 (1986): 46–68; "Role of Stress in the Development of the Hyperventilation Syndrome," *Psychotherapy and Psychoanalysis,* 33 (1980): 214–225; "Breathing Retraining: A Rational Placebo?" *Clincial Psychology Review,* Vol. 12 (1992): 141–153; "Agoraphobia and the Hyperventilation Syndrome," *Behaviour Research and Therapy,* 21 (1983): 643–649.

7.   Benedetti, F., "Neurobiological Mechanisms of the Placebo Effect," *The Journal of Neuroscience,* 25 (November 9, 2005): 10390–402; Thompson, Grant W., *The Placebo Effect and Health: Combining Science and Compassionate Care,* Amherst, MA: Prometheus (2005): 42.

8.   _____, "Conscious Expectation and Unconsciuos Conditioning in Analgesic, Motor, and Hormonal Placebo-Nocebo Responses," *The Journal of Neuroscience,* 23 (May 15, 2003): 4315–23.

9.   Siddle, Bruce, "Sharpen the Warrior's Edge: The Psychology and Science of Training," Illinois: PPCT Management Systems: 105.

EXERCISE 38
SQUARE BREATHING

Begin by taking a slow and comfortable breath. See if you can inhale slowly and continuously for three seconds through the nose. Then hold your lungs full for three seconds without adding stress to the body. Be careful to keep the neck and face relaxed. Next, exhale from the mouth for three seconds without collapsing or wheezing. The air should simply exit as if you had a leak. Finally, hold the lungs empty for three seconds.

This method is used in numerous Russian martial arts. I have encountered it in SWAT officers around the world, in personal protection work, in the writings of Bruce Siddle, Dave Grossman, and even in the conditioning approach of Mark Hatmaker. What matters most is that you remember that everyone is different. The square is a loose frame, not a cage to be bound in. Approximate those counts. If the length is adding anxiety, change it. If you need to make that square a rectangle or even a triangle, do it. Trust your feeling and intuition here. You are the world's best expert on you.

Tactical breathing is largely a pre- and post-combat tool, used before such stress peaks as:

- A SWAT officer preparing to storm a hostile house with his team
- A soldier before engaging
- A prison guard before entering a cell inhabited by a violent inmate
- Someone who has noticed he is being followed and can feel his stress levels skyrocketing
- A student preparing to take an exam in school
- Anyone who trains in the combative arts who wishes to experience the breath effects of combat stress and learn to prepare himself to recover from it

Square breathing can also be used post-combatively to help you regain control over your emotions and to help you debrief and deconstruct a violent encounter. This can also help you regain emotional control after a crisis and reframe the experience, which can be a key factor in whether or not you experience post-traumatic stress.

Inhale through the nose.

Exhale through the mouth.

EXERCISE 39
RECOVERY BREATHING

Sometimes you will find it difficult to stretch the breath into a full square. Despite your best efforts, you will find yourself short of breath. In these instances, it is helpful to use a recovery breath. Do one of the following:

• Simply take a deep inhale through the nose and then *whoosh* the air out by the mouth.

• Take a series of short, sipping inhales, and short, sharp exhales. This technique is commonly used by firefighters. It can be performed either by sniffing in-in-in, then out-out-out, or by in-out, in-out. Inhales should be sharp, like you might do if you were sniffing a mildly runny nose. Exhales should be sharp like you were blowing out a candle. The exhale should *never* be spitty, wheezy, or puffing, as this lack of control in the shape of your lips will encourage a loss of control over the exhale and can contribute to creating strain and tension in the throat and/or chest. Weak exhales linger. Strong, sharp exhales terminate immediately and expunge carbon dioxide more quickly.

As a rule, try to breathe in small bursts two or three times and then return to long, full breathing. If your breathing is still labored, try one or two bursts again and then try to return to normal breathing. If we breathe in bursts too much, we are effectively imitating the symptoms of hyperventilation. Recent studies suggest that imitating the symptoms can in turn trigger panic.[10] Some people overbreathe regularly without suffering from panic. Others seem to be triggered by the appearance of panic.

EXERCISE 40
IDEAL AND RECOVERY STATES

Get into your combat stance. You can stay static, gesturing only with your hands, or move your feet completely like a boxer. Inhale as you move and then exhale long and comfortably as you attack with a salvo of hits. Allow the movement created by you hitting to punctuate your exhale. If your normal exhale would make a steady sound (e.g., "shhhhhhhhhhhh) when you strike three times during your exhale, there should be three punctuations (e.g., "shhhh-sh-sh-sh). After your hit, step back and inhale; then when you are ready to hit, enter and fire off a combo again on the exhale. Eventually, you will find yourself running out of breath. When this happens, step back, keeping yourself safe, and use your recovery breaths to regain control, taking two to three sharp bursts and then testing your ability to return to long breaths.

10. Garssen, B.R., "Breathing Retraining": 141–153.

Burst-sip inhalation.

Burst exhalation.

This photo and those on the following page show me breathing while hitting.

S E C T I O N

4

In a fight, distance can disappear in an instant. Our grasp reflex leaves us snatching blindly at each other, desperate to close the distance and hold on until sense can be made of the chaos and a strategy formulated. Anything that can serve as a handle is twisted, ripped, and wrenched, from cloth to ears to hair. Next, we will look at some clinching fundamentals.

CLINCHING

BREAKING STRUCTURE

As bipods, we are perpetually in a state of imbalance, stumbling toward that missing third point of support that would give us stability—our so-called *triangle point*. As Moshé Feldenkrais first noted, we carry our centers of gravity far above a narrow base. A 6-foot-tall man has a center of gravity roughly 3 feet above the ground but has a base that occupies roughly only 1 foot of surface area in his narrowest natural stance. His center-to-base ratio is therefore 3:1. By comparison, a horse standing 12-feet high, with a center of gravity at 6 feet, can easily occupy a surface area of 12 feet, giving it a ratio of 1:2—a far more balanced proportion. Likewise, the horse will typically carry its heaviest portion along the center band of its body, with its neck and limbs jutting from its center. A human will typically carry his heavy head at the very top of a long, thin lever, followed by heavy shoulders and in some cases an ample midriff—all well above the body center.[1]

As bipods, we have two choices for improving balance. The first is to widen our base, which simultaneously lowers our center of gravity. If we return to our previous example, simply parting our feet can easily bring our center down 6 inches and massively increase our base from 1 foot of surface area to 4 feet, bringing our ratio from a precarious 3:1 to a more respectable 1:4. Through flexion and readiness, we can also increase our ability to explode in linear paths from a lower base, most easily forward since the majority of our muscles are evolved for this purpose.

The second way we can maintain balance is through rotation. As bipods, humans can most easily rotate along their vertical axis, or what is termed the *horizontal plane*—think Linda Carter in the classic *Wonder Woman* TV show. If you simply stand still with your arms outstretched in a T-position and twist your waist and pivot your legs, a healthy individual can easily span 180 degrees with the fingertips. The pirouette of a dancer is a good example of how effectively the human body is able to spin on this plane. By comparison, we are less capable of rotating on our medial plane (like when we backflip or forward roll). If a healthy individual stretches both arms out in front of himself, he will likely be able to touch his toes in front, but few can arch back and touch the ground behind them. Our least comfortable plane is our frontal plane (like when we cartwheel). While some individuals can reach to either side and touch the ground with one hand, few can do this without flexing the support leg and only a small minority of skilled athletes can touch with both hands, usually by raising into a handstand.

BASELINE

The first principle of breaking structure is to seek small incremental changes rather than a single massive movement. This is best done by imagining an invisible line running between your subject's heels. This is what we refer to as the *baseline*. Pressure that runs along the baseline is likely to disrupt balance and cause the aggressor to stumble without necessarily falling. Practice pushing your training partner in all directions. Pushes that intersect your partner's baseline can usually be negated by simply twisting at the hips or shoulders (horizontal plane rotation) or by taking a single backward step (the medial plane). Pushes that run along the baseline are the hardest to absorb, as they will require absorption on the frontal plane (our least adept plane of movement).

---

1.   Feldenkrais, Moishe, *Higher Judo* (reprint), Berkley, CA: Blue Snake Book, 2010.

EXERCISE 41
BASELINE

Practice simply feeling the difference between pushing a partner *through* his baseline and pushing him *along* his baseline. Notice how pushes that work with the baseline move the subject by stumbling him whereas pushes that intersect his baseline challenge his height and threaten to drop him toward his triangle point.

Begin in a stable position.

Push through the baseline to his triangle point.

Aggressor falls to the ground.

Pushing on the baseline causes the subject to stumble.

Exercise 41: normal stance.

EXERCISE 42
GIRAFFE WRESTLING

Lean in toward your partner and touch the crown of your head against his so that your heads are pressed against each other. For an added challenge, you can cross your arms behind your back. Begin to wrestle. Take turns turning perpendicular to one another so that the crown of your head is spearing into his ear. It is extremely important to maintain contact at all times and to push and grind. A failure to do so can result in small bumps and knocks that can easily split the skin and injure the face. For this reason, ear guards or boxing headgear may be worn along with a mouthpiece. In time, the drill can evolve from taking turns to a free competition where both participants are simultaneously trying to side spear their partner with their crown.

This exercise is fantastic for cultivating an intuitive understanding of protecting and using the head in a clinch. It illustrates how to maintain pressure and shows a very direct way to achieve and affect the baseline.

Exercise 41: wider stance and lower center for balance.

Begin crown to crown.

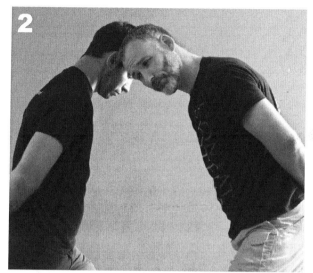

Wrestle to slip to the outside.

Drive perpendicular.

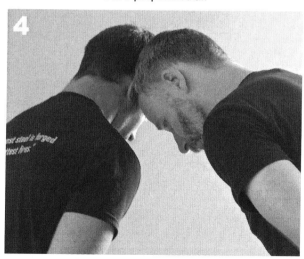

Close-up of perpendicular drive.

The Underhook and Pike

Begin the first essential clinch position by facing your opponent. Place your right arm underneath his left armpit. Reach up with the pads of your fingers and pull the muscle of his deltoid back and down. Keep your thumb and fingers together in what we term a "monkey hand" grip. This is your underhook.

Next, place your left hand on the left side and back of your opponent's neck. You may wish to work with a monkey hand or spread the thumb and drive it into the nerves on the side of his neck. This is your pike. Push the head away strongly while you pull his deltoid in the opposite direction.

This separation/traction illustrated is an essential factor in controlling your assailant.

The aggressor's arm may either be squeezed in the cradle created between your biceps and forearm, or rested on your shoulder and squeezed between your shoulder and head depending on preference and your relative height. In either case, make sure that you squeeze the arm between two surfaces to keep it firmly in place. It is important to keep your

Close-up of the first shoulder cradle and head pinch.

Close-up of second option elbow cradle.

You can deliver short strikes with the forearm anytime.

subject's head lower than his elbow. In the case of resistance, driving knee strikes directly into the side of his thigh or his pubis will usually cause him to buckle. Knees should be launched directly from the ground, without chambering or huge preparation. Knee strikes should fly directly into the target and then return to the ground close to the subject's leg rather than returning to their launch position. Think of stepping past the leg in a large V pattern. Knees with the left leg should land to the left of the target thigh, and knees strikes with the right leg should land on the right. Without breaking contact with the neck, you can also deliver short jolts with your pike into the side of the subject's neck, impacting his nerves. Be wary about sacrificing your balance and trying to knee the face.

A common criticism is that the attacker has

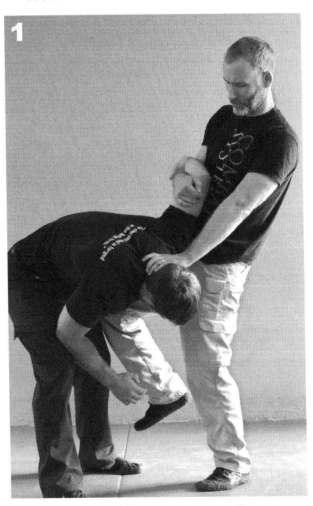

You can deliver knees as you walk.

After striking with the right knee, step forward in a V to the right . . .

a hand free to strike you. This is due to a misunderstanding of the position. If you are correctly aligned on the side of the attacker, keeping his shoulder in a state of traction and his arm sandwiched, and you have his head plunged, he will be unable to reach you with his free arm. It is helpful to block your groin area with your aggressor's head, keeping it constantly in the way of any strikes he might attempt. If needed, drive him downward until he needs to use his free arm to brace himself on surrounding objects or the ground.

Subject attempts to punch your groin.

. . . and knee with the left, always driving forward.

Block by driving his head to the triangle point.

Variations can include replacing your pike hand with the crown of your head as illustrated in the previous Giraffe Wrestling drill and using the freed hand to address the far arm or to strike. The importance of the underhook and pike is that it places the defender on the far side of the attacker and gives the former easier access to the latter's baseline.

An alternate grip with a head spear and a free hand to grab his far arm.

Stand beside your subject.

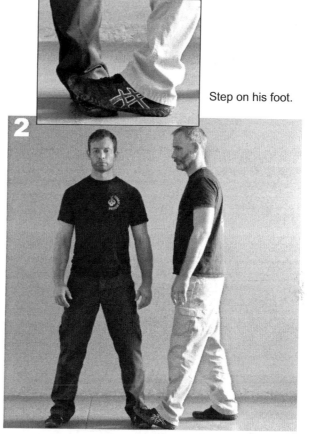

Step on his foot.

EXERCISE 43
STRETCHING THE BASELINE

Beyond stumbling an aggressor along his baseline, another highly effective tactic is to stretch the baseline. We have seen that a common way to improve balance is to simultaneously widen the base while lowering the center. Naturally, there are comfortable limits to how far a base can stretch. Anything beyond that will cause the attacker to fall directly. Simple ways of stretching the baseline include:

• Stand on the nearer foot and shove the opponent briskly along his baseline. By comparison, stepping onto his far foot and pushing will cause a destructive stumble that will cause the attacker to cross his legs and fall easily.

• A less destructive variation is to simply post your foot inside the opponent's near foot and push. There is a chance the attacker will remove his foot during the stumble, but it is still sufficient to disrupt and set up other tactics.

Push him on the baseline.

- Hook and sweep the close leg toward you.

You have the option to block inside his foot.

Push him to split the base with the inside block.

Hook the near leg.

Stretch the baseline.

Replace hook on the ground.

- Kick out the far leg away from you.

Preparing to stretch the baseline.

Kick the far leg.

Destroy the far leg to stretch the base.

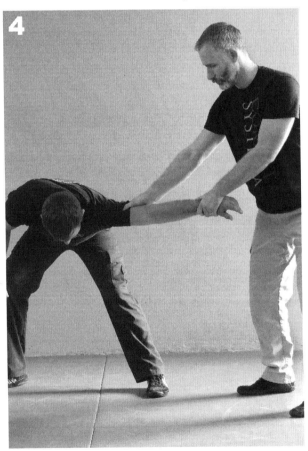

The subject stumbles wider.

EXERCISE 44
VOID AND DENSITY

The moment we begin to affect the baseline, we cause the attacker's weight to shift. To best appreciate this, let's exaggerate this to one end of the spectrum, with the attacker off balance and standing completely on one leg. The floating free leg is what we refer to as a "void." The support leg he is standing on is what we refer to as a "density." A third and final basic principle of manipulating the baseline is that force to a void is more likely to produce a softer sweep while force to a density is more likely to be destructive. We sweep voids and destroy densities.

Practice creating voids and densities from the obvious to the subtle in your partner. Prioritize sweeping and blocking his void side for the most effortless takedowns. Emulate striking his densities to help visualize simple destructions.

Push to create a void on the near leg.

Sweep the void.

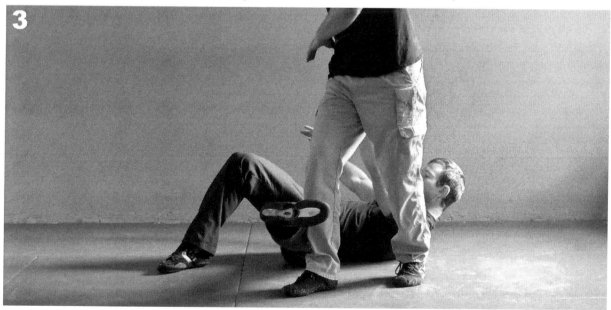

Subject falls to the ground.

Pull subject onto his near leg.

Then knee-strike to destroy the density.

EXERCISE 45
REVIEW

Now let's review through visualization. You are faced with an imminent attack. You preemptively fire off a finger whip, causing your attacker to raise his hands in pain and turn away from you, exposing his baseline. You hammer through his raised hand, batting it down and snaking your arm underneath his armpit, latching onto the back of his deltoid. Before he can adjust, you tug him toward you, spearing the crown of your head into his face. It stuns him completely, and you push him along his baseline, driving knee strikes into his thigh. You can feel your knee impacting his femur through the muscle. He groans, stumbling in pain, and before he can recover, you shove him further onto his far foot, precariously stacking all his weight on that leg for an instant. You drive a final knee into his load-bearing leg. He buckles instantly and falls, writhing in pain.

ANGULATION

The second principle of breaking structure is angulation. Imagine someone grabbed you by the wrist, pulled your arm until it was level with your shoulder, and yanked you forward. You would twist from the hips and shoulders when pulled lightly and, at worst, take a step or two forward like a dog being walked on a leash on harder pulls. You might lean forward from the hips for a moment, but you would be able to recover your structure quite easily. This is because the human body has evolved to move in primarily a forward direction, countering the effects of gravity. If by contrast your arm was allowed to hang straight down and you were pulled by the wrist directly toward your foot, you could resist a considerable amount of effort simply by maintaining the natural alignment of your body or by flexing and absorbing with the knees. You would barely lose any alignment at all.

Pull parallel to the ground.

Pulling toward the subject's triangulation point.

Now imagine that your arm is pulled away from your body at a 45-degree angle, to a point 3 feet in front of you on the ground. Your body would now be likely to both bend at the waist and step forward. You would have the least amount of structural resistance to this type of pressure. In this variation, your head would change height, temporarily shaking the vestibu-lar fluids in your ears and interrupting your eyes' reference point on the horizon line—two integral elements in your balance. If you were to repeat these three angles to the side of your body or to-ward the back, the same relationship would prove constant, with each direction becoming progressively harder to resist and requiring the body to twist and turn in order to adapt.

EXERCISE 46
TRIANGULATION

An easy way to visualize angulation is to return to this idea that, as bipods, we are perpetually seeking a third point of support—our *triangle point*. Working softly with a partner, practice moving him first level with the planet, then directly down into the planet, and finally in all directions on roughly a 45-degree angle. It can be helpful to close your eyes when working on angles initially to help you feel the imbalance you are creating. Work slowly enough that you are able to predict with reliability where your partner will step to counterbalance your effort. Due to the structure of your body, you are most likely to step directly forward in line with your hip, straight to the side, or straight back. Stepping at angles is far less natural.

In truth, any downward 45-degree pressure will create the greatest change in the height of your subject. Ideally, however, it is best you pull or push your partner toward a point that is roughly 3 feet in front or behind him if you are working against his hips or 6 feet if you are working against his head and shoulders. Pressure in line with the toes and heel is easier to adjust to than pressure that inter-sects the center of the baseline, since this requires the leg to step diagonally into a less stable and less familiar position. Be sure to work slowly and carefully with your partner at first to prevent injuries. Matted surfaces are ideal for this exercise.

He stumbles on the baseline.

Steer the subject by his head in all directions.

Pull him down to his triangulation point.

EXERCISE 47
THE BASEBALL BAT GRIP

The rudimentary "baseball bat grip" is ideal for demonstrating triangulation. Standing in front of your partner, firmly grab his wrist with both hands, one on top of the other, exactly as you would a baseball bat. This type of position can manifest quite naturally during grappling, particularly when a knife or stick is involved and control of a single hand is urgent. To maximize this position, keep your elbows tightly anchored against your own body and your opponent's wrist in the space between the two of you. Drive the crown of your head into your partner's face and pull against this anchor to keep his arm in a state of traction. To employ triangulation, simply drop your hips, flexing your knees as if you were performing a sharp squat, and jerk his hand toward his triangle point. A small jolt will usually drop the aggressor to one knee. A more determined drop can be used to drive his hand into the ground, damaging his fingers and wrist.

Baseball bat grip.

Head spear.

Pull to triangulation point.

Destroy the hand.

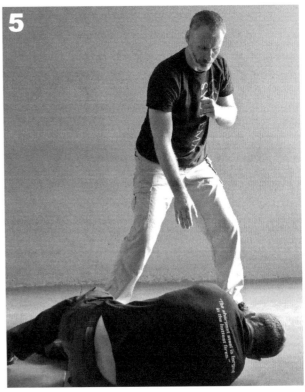

Finish.

The first time I faced a knife, I was sucker punched to the ground while clearing a small group of suspicious loiterers out of a bathroom. I was dazed and recovered a few hits later, finding myself inverted on my back between a toilet and the wall of the stall, piston kicking instinctively upwards against frantic stabs. That was the first time I saw the knife, a quick flash of steel that sent a current of panic through my veins. I managed to get a baseball bat grip on the client's arm and climbed my way up onto one knee, yanking him downward into the frame of the stall and then fully up, driving him back into the counter where I was able to finish him off. It was far from beautiful but it was a perfect example of triangulation.

LEVERAGE

"Give me a lever and a place to stand and I can move the world."

—Archimedes

Levers are one of the six classic machines identified by Renaissance scientists. Consisting of a rod and a fixed hinge/fulcrum, levers allow you to amplify force to lift and move a load. The two most important details to remembering about applying leverage are:

1. The longer the lever, the more mechanical advantage you gain.
2. Fulcrums don't move.

To understand these principles in action on the human body, start by working against the spine. As we have seen, the spine consists of three arches: the cervical arch of the neck, the thoracic round of the shoulders, and the lumbar curve of the lower back. The cervical arch is the most flexible and mobile portion of the spine, the thoracic is the most stable because of the support of the ribs, and the lumbar carries the greatest load. When working against these respective parts, a common error is to smother the arch and in effect choke the lever. For example, practitioners will often place their hand on the nape of their partner's neck when they are trying to bend it, in effect supporting the bulk of

Poor leverage: short lever.

Good leverage: long lever.

the arch. It is far more effective to place the hand near the collar, at the base of the cervical arch. Similarly, when working against the thoracic arch, rather than placing a bracing hand on the round of the shoulder blades, it would be more effective to contact the base of the shoulder blade. Finally, attacks targeting the lumbar arch should focus near the belt or slightly below at the base of the curve rather than resting in the middle of the lower back.

A second common error in applying leverage is to force equally with both points of contact. Returning to the previous example, practitioners will generally try to simultaneously force inward in a scissoring action with both hands, pushing inward on both the front of the head and the back. While this may work in some cases, it is never efficient. If you were trying to jack up your car to change a tire, you wouldn't try to move your jack as you were trying to lift your car—you would only move the jack handle. In exactly the same way, if you are trying to block the back of your opponent's spine, it would be far more efficient to think of pushing him from the front, over your fulcrum hand, and to simply hold your fulcrum firmly in place as an obstacle, rather than trying to also push inward with the fulcrum. Fulcrums do not move. At first, this concept can seem counterintuitive because most of us are prone to forcing with everything. Training softly and slowly to erode excess effort and focus on efficiency is the only way to expose the efficiency of freezing your fulcrum and then training it into your habits.

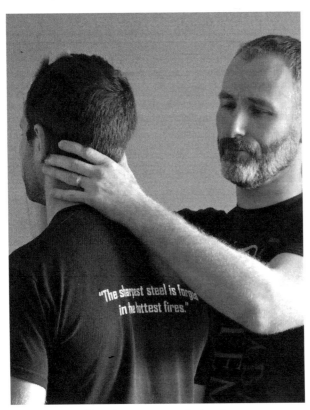

Poor leverage, cervical arch.

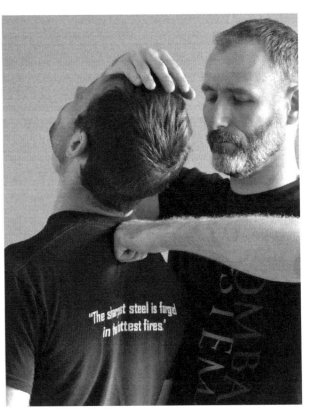

Maximizing cervical arch.

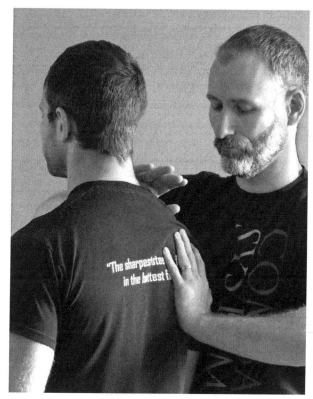

Poor thoracic leverage.

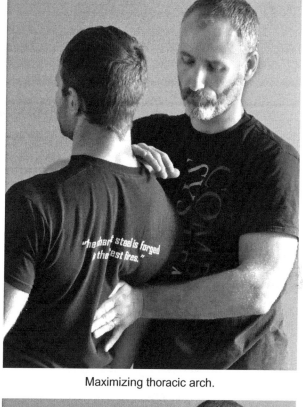

Maximizing thoracic arch.

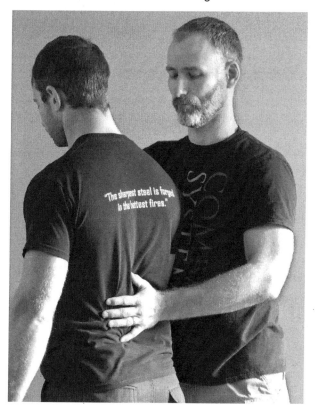

Blocking lumbar leverage.

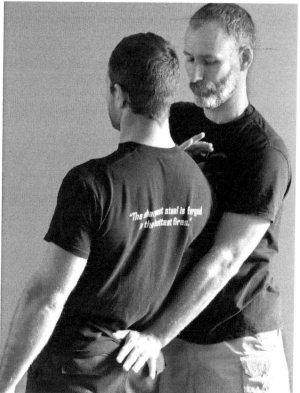

Maximizing lumbar arch.

EXERCISE 48
THE RUSSIAN 2-ON-1 ARM TIE

To understand the next essential clinching position, begin with a baseball bat grip on your partner's hand. Climb up with your top hand to grab just above his elbow, securely latching on to the base of his triceps. Your arms should be naturally positioned as if you were holding a shotgun—never cross them. Remember to keep the crown of your head firmly spearing into your partner's face. This position is known as the Russian 2-on-1 arm tie. The two primary concerns when neutralizing an arm are, first, to prevent it from retracting and, second, to use it to climb toward or around your partner. Moving one hand up from the baseball bat grip to the Russian 2-on-1 facilitates both.

Russian 2-on-1 arm tie.

Acquisition of baseball bat grip with head spear.

Climb up to acquire 2-on-1 tie.

Doing so makes you vulnerable to his punches.

Preferable outside 2-on-1.

The body and head are more difficult to reach.

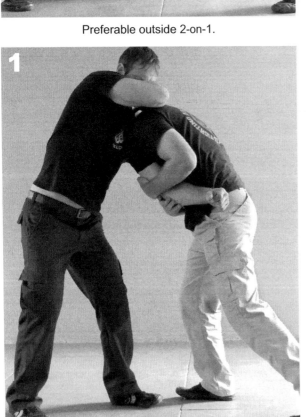

Options include transferring elbow grip.

Then grab the leg to begin climbing behind the attacker.

Reverse angle view of leg grab.

Grabbing the hip.

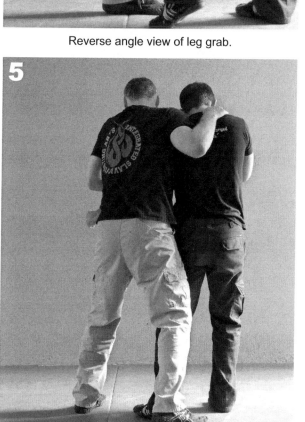

Grabbing the trapezius muscle.

Reverse angle of the trapezius grab.

EXERCISE 49
THE RODEO DRILL

Begin in a baseball bat grip. When you are ready, have your partner start working to retract his arm. He can use his free hand to try to pull your grips off, move your head spear, shoot for your legs, or push or pull you in any other way that might serve him. Your goal is to study how and when you are able to climb one hand up above his elbow to achieve a 2-on-1 arm tie during his resistance. Depending on your initial baseball bat grip, either hand may be on top, resulting in your achieving the arm tie either inside (with your back toward the attacker's free hand) or outside (farther away from his free hand, which is preferable).

As an added challenge, prioritize arriving on the outside when you find yourself inside. Here's how you can do this. If you have baseball-gripped your partner's right arm with your own right hand on top, when you climb up with your right hand to his triceps, you will be on the inside of his body. Your partner will be able to hit you easily with his free hand. To switch positions, drive forward with both hands, jamming the trapped arm against the attacker's own body and take a step to the left with your left foot. Release your left-hand grip of his wrist and pull his arm with your right hand up underneath your right armpit. From this point, your left hand is free to reach for his leg, belt, hip, neck, and a host of other handles. To return to a 2-on-1 on the outside, simply reinsert your left arm underneath his triceps to block its retraction and then slip your right hand slightly down to his wrist.

Inside Russian 2-on-1 tie.

Drive your arm into the subject's body.

Switch to the outside grip.

EXERCISE 50
WEAPONIZING THE RUSSIAN 2-ON-1

A very simple way to practice weaponizing the Russian arm tie is to begin in an outside grip with your partner holding a focus mitt in his free hand. Here are some basic ideas to drill:

Head spearing the mitt.

- Have your partner place the back of his free hand on his closer cheek so that you can spear firmly into his focus mitt. For safety, you should both wear mouthpieces. Practice driving and grinding with your head into the pad. You may also wish to deliver small jolts. I am not an advocate of delivering large head butts where your head swings to any degree because this will swish your brain around the inside of your skull like the family pet in a car accident. Instead, I promote keeping the neck braced in perfect alignment and delivering small micro-spears with an inch of distance at most. This will not damage you in any way or affect your brain or balance but will cause the recipient to temporarily forget a few years of math. In the same way, I've had tremendous success with a move I refer to as "match-lights," which is when you slide your crown briskly from one position to another, as if your head were a match and your partner's face were the matchbook.

- Have your partner hold the focus mitt against his near-side ribs. Practice temporarily releasing control of your elbow grip to deliver short punches or palm strikes to the ribs. It is important that your arm stays relatively in the same spot to continue blocking his ability to retract his arm. You can also play with maintaining your grip while delivering short elbows to the ribs.

- Have your partner hold the focus mitt over his solar plexus on a downward angle. Practice temporarily releasing control of your wrist grip to deliver hook punches or palms to the plexus or face.

- Throw the focus mitt down on the ground near but not on your partner's foot. Practice delivering powerful foot stomps to the mitt while maintaining control of the arm to simulate stomping his foot.

Hook punching the ribs.

Hook punching the plexus.

Stomping the foot.

Single Nape Control

The next essential clinching position to explore is neck control. The most essential neck control, the single nape, is achieved by placing one hand directly behind a partner's head. You perform the first variation, the inside single nape, by grabbing the head directly, with your right hand extending to the left side of the aggressor's head or vice versa. The most common mistake again is to choke the lever and brace the neck with your hand. Instead, align your little finger with the base of your partner's skull so that the neck is fully exposed and your fingers are cupping the base of the skull. This is about as far up the head you can go without sacrificing a solid grip. Plant your elbow into your partner's chest or the front of his shoulder. This will be your fulcrum against which you can lever his head forward. It will also help control your partner and prevent him from moving forward into a counterclinch.

The second variation of the single nape is achieved by reaching diagonally across the aggressor, with your left hand extending to the right side of the head or vice versa. The outside nape grip is generally preferable in non-sportive encounters since it keeps the majority of the attacker farther away from your body. When performing an inside single nape, it is important to make every effort to push the aggressor to one side and keep your body perpendicular to his rather than remaining flush with him.

The single nape is quick to acquire. It is often

Outside single nape.

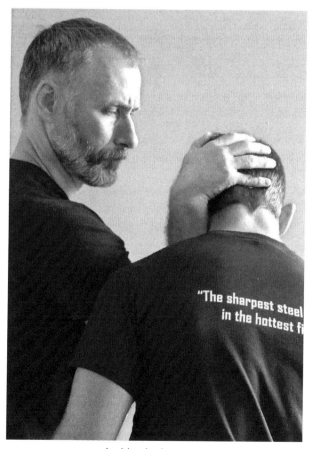

Inside single nape.

noted how the head is like a steering wheel. Wherever you move it, the body will follow. This makes nape control an excellent strategy that leaves one hand free to control the attacker's arms, to counter strike, or to access weapons.

Single nape control also allows you to push your way into your attacker's corner flank or side. This makes it a great transitional position from which to move behind him. It is also a great striking position, since it allows you to stay away from your opponent's far hand, smother his close hand, and achieve superior angles for your own attacks.

EXERCISE 51
EXPLORING CONTROL

Practice softly acquiring the single nape on your partner. It can be used like a joystick to push and pull him forward and back, and side to side. Study the different effects created by stumbling your partner on his baseline from nape control versus pulling him to his triangle point, versus simply levering his head forward and crimping his neck.

Next, practice plunging the aggressor's head downward slightly and pivoting your hand to the opposite side of the head, converting your inside nape grab to an outside grip. This type of quick switch can be done while maintaining arm control with the free hand, while striking or accessing a weapon.

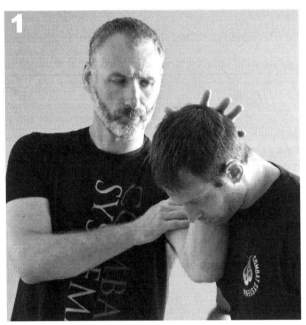

Push your subject away with a single nape.

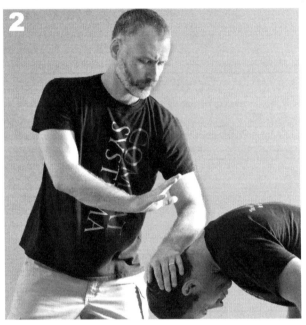

Plunge his head down . . .

. . . and snake it to the opposite side.

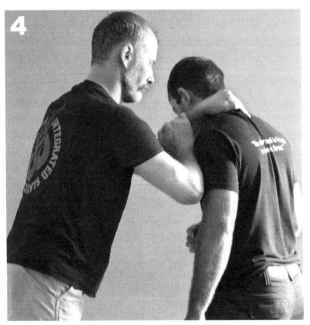

Arrive in outside single nape with the same arm.

Begin with the single nape.

Close the open side, tucking the
subject's head into your shoulder.

An alternate view of the tuck.

Double Nape Control

Sometimes, it may be preferable to use double nape control. To achieve this, begin with inside single nape control and simply add your second arm on the far side. It is important to note that in a double nape control, both arms are not necessarily symmetrical. One arm is usually fully bent in a single nape control, and the second is somewhat straighter and simply serving to close the open side. This is largely owing to the fact that most people lack the flexibility to crane both elbows in symmetrically. Moreover, a fully symmetrical position would place you squarely in front of your aggressor and, as we know, we would always prefer to be zoned to one angle, which in this case requires an arm to be dominant. Your hands should simply overlap for greatest speed, ease, and strength. Do not interlock your fingers. Simply overlap one over the other across the base of the skull.

Double nape control is generally used when you want to drive the opponent's head completely down to smother his mechanical capacities, often while delivering low line attacks with kicks and the knees.

EXERCISE 52
GRABBING THE BULL BY THE HORNS

Like the rodeo drill, begin with the position already acquired—in this case, with you holding a double nape. Ideally, have your partner wear boxing gloves and begin gently throwing hooks and uppercuts to your body. Study how you are able to plunge his head down and jerk it from side to side to unbalance him and thwart his attempts. Evolve to moving freely from double to single nape control as your partner increases his intensity and includes groin hits and overhand hooks to your head. Remember, this is an isolation drill that exaggerates and prolongs a sliver of potential combat. In a real situation, you would not choose to dwell in this position for long, but isolation and pressure testing of every segment are necessary for improving your overall performance.

ALIGNMENT

The fourth consideration in breaking structure is an understanding of alignment. We have seen that we are unstable two-legged creatures who have evolved for movement and dynamic balance. This depends on efficient alignment—our bones are designed to be correctly stacked, with our connective tissue holding everything together and our muscles providing pull. A basic rule of breaking structure, therefore, is to steal this alignment and always try to keep your opponent bent or crooked. The underhook and pike combo is so effective partly because one arm is pulled away from the body, the head is pushed out of alignment, and the body is bent forward. The baseball bat grip achieves the same effects. When performing a Russian arm tie, you massively isolate your opponent's arm. Through it, along with work against his baseline and triangulation point, the defender is constantly stumbling to return to form. The single nape crimps and deforms the neck. In everything you do, ask, "Could I be deforming my partner more?"

Basic head control on your attacker.

Roll with his punches.

Aggressively steer his head to control him.

4

Pin his head low.

EXERCISE 53
ALIGNMENT POWER TEST

Stand on the outside of your partner. Have him place one arm outstretched at shoulder height with the palm facing the sky. Slowly apply pressure to begin pushing his arm down to his waist. He should resist as much as possible. Notice how much force is required for you to succeed. Take a breath. Now, have your partner place one ear on his shoulder and keep it there while maintaining his outstretched arm. Repeat the drill. Notice the massive lack of power in his resistance now. This is a very simple exercise that illustrates the direct correlation between power and alignment. In everything you do, seek to steal your attacker's alignment and power while maximizing yours. I am always reminded of a good friend of mine who was distracted by a beautiful girl walking by while performing his bench press. He just crumpled like a paper cup.

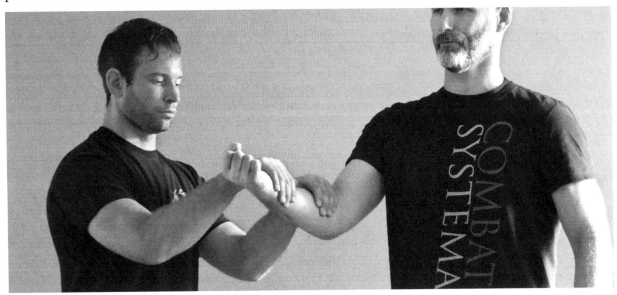
Resisting arm pressure with correct alignment.

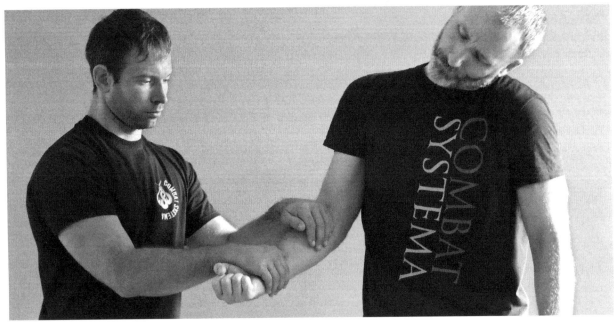
Resisting arm pressure with poor alignment robs you of power.

ATTACKING THE NERVOUS SYSTEM

The martial arts are replete with myths and misunderstanding revolving around pressure points and pain compliance. Susceptibility varies. Alcohol, drugs, and heightened emotions can all negate the effects of pain. Pain is not reliable, and so naturally I do not believe in basing a system on it. Pain is a bonus. It's the cherry on top of the sundae. Pain is nonetheless important because it can deform structure. I remember once getting smacked so hard I needed to get a root canal on a tooth. The day after getting hit, I woke up feeling like a bowling ball was dangling off the nerve in my tooth. That simple little pain crumpled me up like an old man and made walking and standing very difficult. A little bit of pressure on one nerve had destroyed me.

Attacking the nervous system by raking the fingers across the sensitive tissue of the eyes, nose, and lips.

EXERCISE 54
HIDDEN STRIKES

Strikes, gouges, rakes, and twists can be delivered from any position. It must be remembered that any clinching position is just a delivery mechanism. It is the vehicle we use to improve our position, protect ourselves, and deliver counterstrikes. Your creativity is your only limit. To help get your juices flowing, here are just a few ideas from simple nape control.

- When the opponent's hair is long enough, grabbing and pulling it is an excellent tactic. When possible, grabbing closer to the crown is best, since this gives you the longest lever and greatest mechanical advantage. The crown can be pulled downward on a 45-degree angle to the front or back.

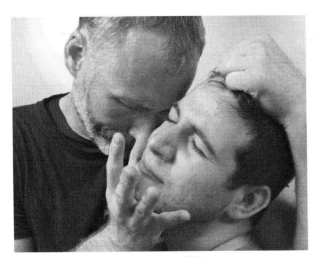

Pulling your opponent's hair can be an excellent tactic.

- When pulling on the ears, wedge your fingertips as deeply as you can behind the ear and clamp in tightly toward your palm. There is a very real danger of ripping the ear off, so if you wish to minimize this risk, it is preferable to reach around the back of the subject's head for the far ear. In the second instance, push the ear forward with the palm of your hand and then clamp your fingertips down through the ear into your palm. Pull in a circular manner as if you were trying to turn the opponent's nose to the back of his head. This will give you good control while deferring some of the direct stress on the ear itself.

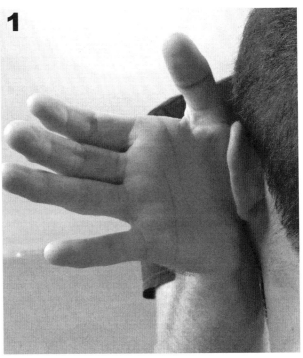

Open hand near the ear.

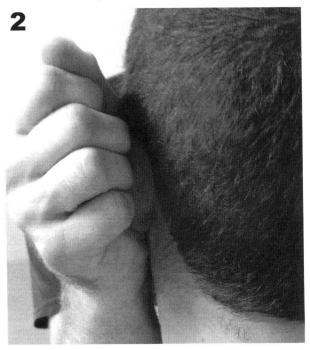

Closing and peeling the ear between
the finger pads and palm.

• From nape control, move your shoulder up and forward in a rolling action as you pull briskly on your partner's head to strike with the shoulder to the face or throat. This is a surprising hit that delivers a dense and heavy shot. This also helps you keep your face safely to one side and somewhat shielded by the subject's head.

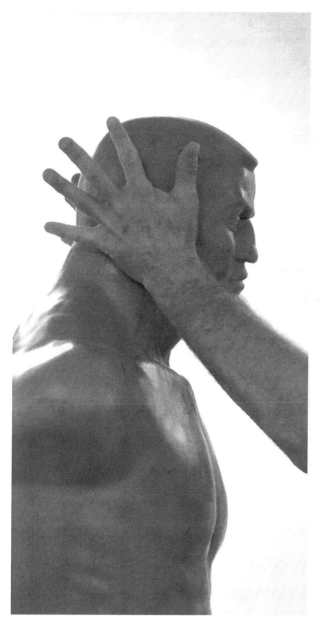

Slapping the ears.

Nape grab.

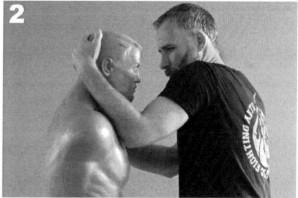

Loading the shoulder.

Striking the face with the shoulder.

Tug your partner's head slightly toward you, bending and "loading" your inner arm. Then, explosively elongate your arm, striking the side of his neck or head with the radial edge of your forearm just below the elbow fold. It is important to screw your thumb from the upward orientation of your nape hold to a downward position, as if you were dumping out a glass. This will both help generate more power via the screwing action and help protect the joint from overextension. A slight forward pivot from the hip is also essential for deeply penetrating into the target. This strike can safely be trained against your partner's shoulder to test its power.

THE BEAR TRAP

Think of a bear trap—an iron jaw, cranked open against powerful springs into a state of frightening tension, ready to slam its fangs shut on any unsuspecting leg that may cross its threshold. The clinching position of the same name is equally menacing. The bear trap is most powerfully applied by swinging the arm around your attacker's neck, as if you were throwing a discus. The hand is kept palm down and ideally you impact the side of the subject's neck with your biceps first and then wrap around, impacting the nape or far side of his neck with your forearm and engulfing him in a powerful headlock. Against taller opponents, aim to impact with the radial edge of your wrist on the side of his neck and grip the back of his neck. The second hand greets the attacker's face with any manner of slam or clawing action to sandwich his head completely. From this position, drive the front clawing hand back over the rear fulcrum arm, jamming the face and chin up slightly, and then twist the opponent's nose powerfully toward the back of his head to steer him aggressively to the ground.

Once, while working at a club, the only other bouncer on staff got into a 4-on-1. When I came in to provide backup, no one noticed me and I pulled the first guy off using a bear trap and threw him away as hard as I could. He did not get back up. I instinctively did it

Begin in a single nape, pulling the head inward.

Extend and spiral the arm.

again on the second guy, again from behind. He just writhed on the ground holding his face. At that point, the other two noticed it was getting chilly without the insulation of their friends around them and they turned. We had a long verbal standoff. As I helped a very hurt buddy back onto his feet, I saw one of the two I had discarded still writhing nearby, and the other had run. Two bear traps had effectively ended it all.

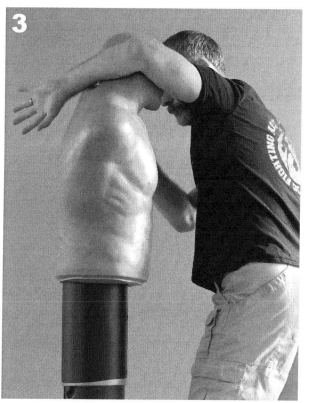

Strike the face and neck with the inner elbow and forearm.

Catch the head, pulling it back inward.

EXERCISE 55
GOOD MEDICINE

You need a partner and a heavy medicine ball. Practice throwing the ball to your partner. Try to catch the ball in a bear trap, absorbing the direct impact with your torso and one palm and whipping your arm around the ball with a leg pivot to move with the force. Pivot back and return the ball. This is a very simple and quick way to develop tremendous power in your bear trap.

Stand in front of your partner, who has a medicine ball.

He throws the medicine ball to you.

Catch the ball with your chest and arms,
like a bear trap, and pivot to absorb the force.

CENTER

The Russian perspective on center of gravity is somewhat different from what is commonly taught in the Asian arts. It is perceived as being in constant flux, residing between the point just below the navel at its lowest (akin to the Asian notion of *hara* or *dantiem*) and the solar plexus. When we are standing naturally or in a stance, our center resides in our lower "lunar plexus." When we are outstretched, particularly as we might be when bent forward shooting a pistol with our arms outstretched, or when we are latched onto someone's clothing and looking to throw him, our total body length stretches and our center effectively rises up closer to our solar plexus. This notion is known as a floating center of gravity.

There are three basic ways people can be moved:

- They can be rotated around their center.
- They can be rotated around your center.
- They can be rotated around both simultaneously.

Example of standard center two inches below the navel.

Example of extended body length wherein the center rises closer to the plexus.

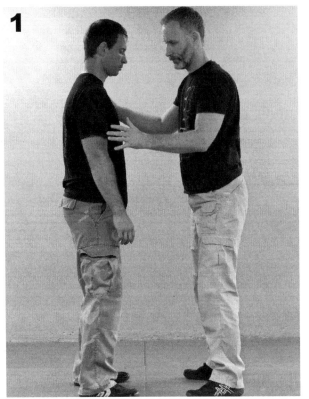

Turn the subject around his center and into a position of control.

Rotate the subject around your center to the far side.

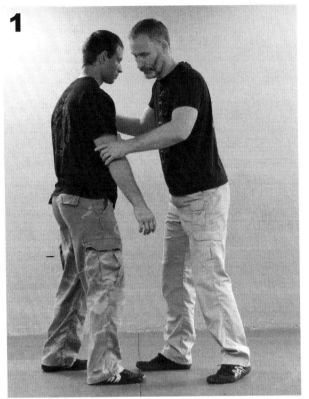

Turn the subject around his center while simultaneously turning him around yours.

EXERCISE 56
CONTROLLING CENTER

Begin with your back against a solid wall with a partner standing in front of you. Practice softly moving your partner around his vertical axis so that you can access his back without moving yourself. For example, you might push on one shoulder while pulling on the other to steer him. Similarly, you could drag one of his arms diagonally across the space between your bodies. A personal favorite is to hook his nose with space between your thumb and index finger and twist his head like you were screwing in a lightbulb. All these tactics are useful when working in very tight spaces, and you need to control your subject or use him as a body shield.

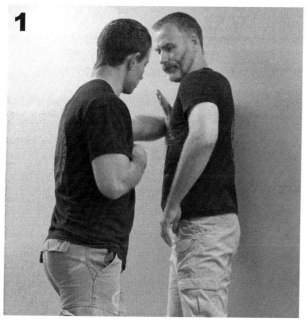
Your partner pushes you while you are against the wall.

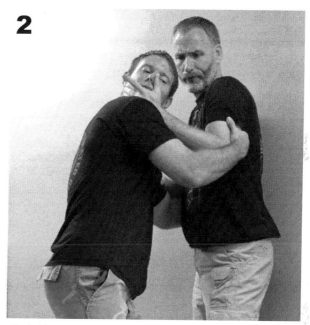
Grab his chin and nose, and twist his face away from you.

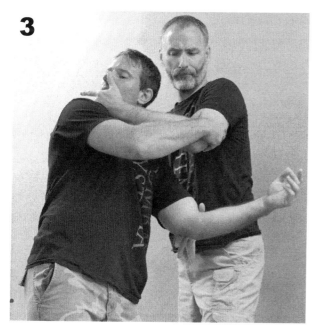
Guide his arm between you with your free arm.

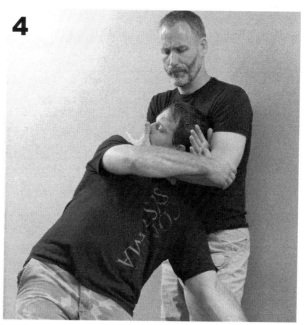
Control his head.

The above would all be examples of moving the subject around his center.

Next, working in an open space, grab your partner firmly and step back, pulling him to the void you have just created. Nape grabs, wrist and arm holds, and body clinches are very effective for this. These would be examples of moving an aggressor around your center.

SECOND OPTION

Use an underhook and strike the neck.

Plunge his head downward while twisting his arm.

Push him to the ground.

Finally, practice doing both, moving the subject around his center and yours simultaneously or in close succession. Any combination of the work above will suffice. Locking up with an aggressor when you have your back to the wall, spinning him to take his back, and then slamming him face-first into a wall to restrain him would be a good example of working around both centers simultaneously.

EYES AND EARS

The final consideration is the role of the eyes and ears in assisting balance and contributing to structure. The vestibular fluids in our ears play an important role in our sense of balance. When the fluid is disrupted, we temporarily lose equilibrium. Any brisk movement of the head achieves this. Also, solid slaps or punches to the ear can accomplish this, while also being extremely painful. The ears are also constantly absorbing sound. The brain processes sound more quickly than sight, so any noise that you make can temporarily startle and disorient your aggressor. Shouting is a well-known tactic for surprising an opponent long enough to enter, but it can be even more devastating up close when you scream into a subject's ear. The ears can adjust quickly, so prolonged or repeated screaming quickly loses effect, but a sudden shouted command at a pivotal moment of resistance can be enough to delay an aggressor's response.

Similarly, the eyes play a huge role in our sense of balance. A commonly repeated myth is that blind people have their remaining senses heightened. Numerous studies have shown this to be false. What in fact occurs is that blind people simply learn to use their remaining senses more effectively and to pay better attention to nuances that we might otherwise ignore. Michael G. Wade and Graeme Jones have shown that vision plays a critical role not only in balance, but also in basic posture.[2] This is easily demonstrated. When most people are blindfolded, their ears are given priority and the eyes are lowered, causing the head to bend forward out of alignment. They also tend to reach out with their arms and lower their center. Under combative stress, the exact same reactions occur. Simply covering someone's eyes will often cause the person to freeze and brace himself. Gouging or tapping him is a double win because it also attacks nerve centers.

The eyes can also be affected. Looking away from the subject can cause him to follow your line of sight. Using natural gesture can cause him to become distracted, and sudden movements can trigger flinches, all of which impair sight.

2.   Wade, Michael G., and Graeme Jones, "The Role of Vision and Spatial Orientation in the Maintenance of Posture," *Physical Therapy* 77 (June 1997): 619–628.

EXERCISE 57
ATTACKING THE SENSES

Lightly wrestle with your partner and explore any of the concepts we have seen so far. Now, actively try to incorporate attacks on the eyes and ears. Some good guidelines are:

- Alternate wrestling both with your eyes closed and blindfolded to see what differences you feel.

Wrestling blindfolded.

- Practice playing with sound. You can slap your body or shout the moment before you make a sudden move to startle your opponent. Again, use this sparingly, or it will lose effect.
- Practice taking a long, seeping exhale as you wrestle for a few rhythms and then punctuate your exhale with a few short bursts. Simply hearing a change in breathing patterns can trigger tension and flinching, and make your partner overreact.
- Practice taking a long, seeping exhale when you sink in a choke. It can induce panic and compliance, both of which assist the choke.
- Talk constantly during practices. Beyond having direct applications for de-escalation efforts, it can be hugely distracting. Consider the glorious levels to which certain individuals, such as Muhammad Ali, have taken trash talking.

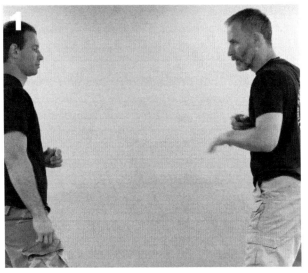

Square off with your opponent.

Shout to startle him.

Immediately launch a finger whip.

- Incorporate slaps and grinding actions to the ears and eyes.

Grinding the eyes.

- Practice faking with your gestures to bait your opponent. As a general rule, fake high and then attack low or vice versa, or move a limb on one line and then attack on another, like twitching your lead hand outward on a lateral line for a moment and then striking straight with a jab.

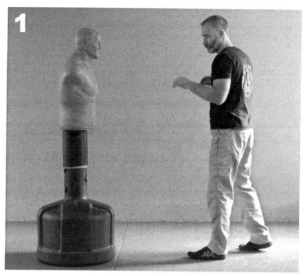

Starting position.

Fake a kick.

Then strike with a finger whip.

REVIEW

I crammed a lot of information in this section, and we will come back to most of it throughout the remainder of this book. The key is to take one concept and drill it until it becomes second nature. You don't need to incorporate all these ideas or to do them in any specific sequence. Anything that you can incorporate will improve your efficiency, and that is enough. To help your recall, I have formatted the material into the acronym BALANCE:

- **B**aseline: you can stumble your opponent on his baseline, stretch it past his comfortable base, or sweep voids and destroy densities.

- **A**ngle: Whenever possible, push or pull on 45-degree angles toward his triangle point.

- **L**everage: Don't choke your lever. Longer levers give you more advantage. Fulcrums don't move. Keep them fixed and apply force around them.

- **A**lignment: Deform your opponent and rob him of his full power whenever possible.

- **N**ervous system: Pressure points and nerve centers are not magic. Don't obsess or rely on them. They are a cherry on top of the sundae.

- **C**enters: You can move your opponent around his center, your center, or both simultaneously.

- **E**yes and ears: Sight and hearing are essential to balance. Disrupt them through any means necessary.

SECTION
5

GROUND FIGHTING

The ground plays an important role in Combat Systema. In my personal experience, real fights often go to the ground, and they can continue there. People can recover. People can also get destroyed there. In restraint settings, the ground is even more essential. I have rarely had a resistant restraint encounter that did not need to go to the ground or at minimum get pressed into a wall or bent over something.

KEY CONCEPTS

The key concepts to remember about ground fighting are as follows:

- You should never choose to go to the ground (ducking to take cover from gunfire being about the only exception I can think of). If you find yourself on the ground, it is because you slipped, were knocked down, or were tackled.

- Although you never want to volunteer for the ground, you do want to be adept there. A lack of familiarity is a hole in your armor and a factory that churns out fear. I have seen many people struggling to put a subject down because they themselves are frightened to go to the ground. It's like trying to drown someone when you don't know how to swim. It is always apparent, and these attempts are rarely successful. You must make the ground your home and be as functional on your back as you are on your knees or your feet.

- If you end up on the ground, the odds are against you. Your justification for increased use of force goes up. Your first goal must be to find the next available instance to stand.

- If you can't move smoothly and fluidly on the ground in your solo work, adding an enraged, drugged-out attacker with a knife is not going to miraculously make you more capable. We don't rise to the occasion—we fall to the level of our training.

EXERCISE 58
GROUND POSTURE

The first step is to learn how to adapt your defensive posture to the ground. To begin, simply sit on the ground with your legs outstretched. Without using your arms, practice lying back. The goal is to lean slightly to one side so that the meat of the back touches the ground, and not the spine. Keep your chin tucked low. As you get lower, you may wish to brace your chin against the bottom shoulder for added support. At first, practice going down and returning on the same side. As this becomes comfortable, practice rolling across the back and coming up on the other side. This is referred to as a "circle sit-up." When rolling across the back, avoid completely rounding the shoulders and exposing the spine. Instead, work to keep the shoulders soft and somewhat together to provide a small space for the spine.

When working against more extreme levels of force, you may wish to allow the hands to touch the ground. It should be noted that this should be done naturally, in a sliding action. Do not slap the ground or add force to the hands.

When on the ground, try to avoid remaining on your back. Staying on one corner will provide greater mobility. Have a standing partner try to get around you. Remain coiled like a snake and pivot on your hip, using your feet and hands as needed to keep your feet oriented toward your attacker. We will address variations for multiple attackers shortly.

Starting sitting position.

Lean to one side, touching the ground with a cupped hand.

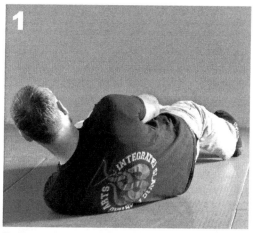

Roll onto your corner without touching the spine.

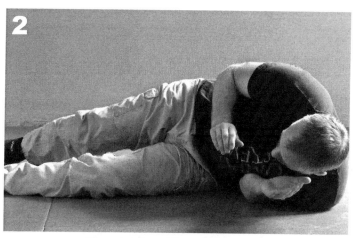

Alternate view of the roll onto corner.

Roll across the back to the far shoulder.

Avoid staying flat on your back.

Sit up.

GROUND RECOVERY

The most common method for returning to your feet is known as the tactical stand. From your corner position, place your bottom hand firmly on the floor, maintaining a slight flexion in your elbow to protect from unseen impacts. Your free lead hand can be used to shield, keep distance, or manipulate a weapon. When you have established that you have enough time to safely stand, plant your top foot on the ground. (**Note:** Because you are on your corner, you will be posting on your bottom hand and top foot.) Raise your hips off the ground and thread your free bottom leg through the frame you have created. Some schools advocate bringing the threaded foot all the way back as close to your support hand as possible. In application, under stress and particularly while wearing heavy equipment, this can be difficult. I suggest prioritizing going to one knee first. This is a safer interim position that allows you to quickly return to the ground if needed. It also allows you to pivot from a three-point stance easily and to stand when it is safe to do so. Less athletic individuals will find transitioning to their knee far easier than trying to stand directly on their foot.

Roll onto corner.

Remain defensive.

Post rear hand, rise onto your rear knee, and twist into a standing position.

EXERCISE 59
RECOVERING UNDER STRESS

Attackers may charge you while you are trying to stand. Here are a few simple drills to help you better prepare for this:

• As you are standing, have your partner shoot in toward you. Use your lead hand to make a frame with the forearm or post your hand on him to temporarily keep him away. Practice standing in the same manner while keeping your distance.

You are in a defensive ground position.

Assume your three-point stance.

3

Intercept your attacker's tackle
by driving your forearm into his neck.

4

Alternate perspective
of head deflection.

5

Steer him to the ground.

- Have your attacker continue to tackle you onto your back while you scissor your legs around him to hold him at bay as you fall. From the guard position, acquire a single nape, pushing yourself to one side of the attacker's head. Place your free hand and diagonal foot on the ground and thread stand out from underneath them. The key is to constantly push your aggressor away from your centerline to relieve the pressure he is applying. Do not fight this force directly and try to stand while in his path. Once you make it to a three-point stance, you can sprawl on his back and shoulders to drive him to the ground or circle out to control him and strike.

From your back, use your legs to control the aggressor.

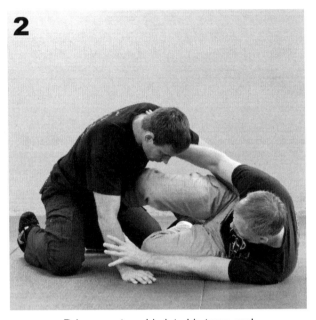

Drive your top shin into his torso and slip your bottom leg away from him.

Post your free knee and hand on the ground to the side of the aggressor.

Drive him to the ground as you stand to his side.

- Imagine your partner tackles you down and bypasses your legs, acquiring a cross mount position. Wedge your forearm against his neck and shoulder, and run out backward to get onto your knees. From there you can counter control and strike back more effectively.

If your opponent passes your legs and cross-mounts, wedge your forearm into his neck.

Bridge your hips.

Roll away from your attacker on your knees.

Standing solidly on your knees, finish with strikes.

MULTIPLE ATTACKERS

In the case of multiple attackers, it will not be possible to safely stay on your back or corner. Practice transforming your circle sit-up and then rolling onto your stomach, bringing your elbows and knees underneath you, arriving in a turtle position. While your goal should be to never stop moving, try to roll as close to the nearest attacker as possible and drive into his legs. Whenever possible, try to tuck your head on the outside of his leg. Drive forward and up, climbing up his body in a spiral.

Avoid staying on your back.

Roll onto your side to protect the organs.

Continue into a turtle position to shield the inner body.

Rise into a three-point stand.

Stand shielded.

As you climb, drive into the attacker's baseline to unbalance him. This will make his nearer leg a void, allowing you to lift it easily as you stand. From this position, you can sweep his void leg to the ground, pass his leg, and attack his body with knees and stomps.

I once survived a rather severe beating in this manner when my backup failed to notice I was in trouble. By the time backup arrived, I was teetering on the verge of unconsciousness and badly bloodied. I was fortunate to have escaped more severe injuries, but the experience left a very clear memory in my psyche. The feeling of helplessness was profound. No matter what I seemed to do, nothing seemed to work at first, but I remained focused on recovering. The reality of the ground is truly fearsome. A single mistake in any fight can cost you survival. When you are grounded, the stakes skyrocket and time evaporates. I reiterate this to stress how important it is to maintain a realistic understanding of the ground. When we find ourselves down, our goal must always be to get back up at all costs.

EXERCISE 60
SURVIVING MOBS

- Beginning on your back, practice having two to four partners stand around you. For the initial phase of work, simply practice moving, circle "sit-upping," rolling, and turtling from person to person. Your partners

Turn as close to one attacker as possible.

Stick to that attacker, climbing up . . .

Practice shielding near static partners.

. . . and unbalancing him as you do so.

should begin by simply standing around you as static obstacles. This allows the practitioner to become comfortable with basic evasive movements and practice safely recovering from the ground.

- For a second phase of study, have your standing partner begin by simply taking a step forward, back, or side to side, churning on the spot slowly. This simple change in position will get the practitioner used to adjusting to a changing dynamic.

- For a third phase of work, have the standing partners begin to step with intention, trying to pin the attacker's limbs and torso to the ground. When the limbs are trapped, emphasize retracting the limbs in a spiral, screwing motion so as to share the load with multiple muscle groups and to most efficiently deflect the pressure applied to them. When pressure is applied to the torso, roll toward the pin, raising the free side to help slip out. This is the same concept that we saw applied in our basic yielding drills, but on the ground. As soon as possible, retract your limbs and get into a turtle position to protect your organs and head.

- For a fourth phase, begin by allowing the attackers to stomp and kick softly. You both should wear shin pads to protect your legs and feet. Allow the pressure of the kicks to influence your movement and, to the best of your ability, yield to the force and find natural openings in the attacks in order to stand.

KNEE ON BODY

The knee pin is an extremely instinctive and common occurrence when an opponent is downed. It involves simply driving one knee into the torso of the defender, bracing the far foot against the ground to help drive into the opponent. The knee pin allows the mounted attacker to rain down strikes and smother and control his arms.

When a knee pin is correctly applied, it is difficult to breathe and move. There is a tendency for many individuals to freeze up, suffering needless hits. A second reflex is to squirm on the ground, but depending on where the knee is placed, struggling may actually worsen your position and open you up to a full mounted position or simply waste energy without improving your situation.

The first step must be to disrupt your attacker's base by bridging. People often regard bridging as simply raising the hips as high as possible, but there are two fundamental keys that we should always seek to incorporate:

1. Don't bridge from the hips; bridge from the tailbone. Have your partner knee-pin you and, despite the pain, slowly curl the tailbone upward to drive your hips as high as you can. This will help you brace your pelvis and will make your legs much stronger and more stable. As we saw in our spinal check, you should also seek to pull the ribs in toward the spine. Again we see that spinal awareness must permeate everything that we do.

2. Try to bridge up onto the balls of the feet (a.k.a. "Russian bridge") rather than on the arches or, worse, the heels. The common tendency when attempting a Russian bridge is to begin in a comfortable flat-footed position and to simply raise the heels. This will generally result in the feet being too far away from the hips. Instead, begin by placing your feet comfortably on the floor. As you activate your tailbone and begin raising your hips, slide the balls of your feet to the spot your heels are occupying. You will notice a huge difference in stability and height since your point of support will be better aligned with the structure of your legs. This is how you should always train to bridge. Practice this in your solo health and mobility work. Add contraction and load. Imprint a deep memory of this correct position into your nervous system.

While this bridge will require some training to become instinctive, it will be one of your most essential basic movements in your repertoire so the payoff is huge. In application against the knee pin, the bridge should be performed as quickly as a sneeze. This will seriously destabilize even much larger attackers. From the bridge position, quickly turn in toward your opponent, pushing with both hands into his knee, thigh, or groin to scrape the pin off you. As the attacker's knee falls to the ground, stay stuck to him. Get onto your knees, driving into your attacker's body and climb up into a superior position.

There is a common tendency to think of simply striking the groin or related dirty shots. By all means, we should attack wherever we can, but dirty striking is not enough. If we have no sense of how to escape and we resort to desperately striking from an inferior position, we may not finish off our attacker and risk escalating aggression. We don't want to simply fight from a bad position—we want to fight toward a better one. Your strikes can also easily be integrated with your push away.

Your partner pins you with his knee on your body.

Bridge with your hips to disrupt his base.

Close-up of bridge.

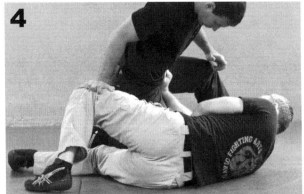

Slip out of his hold to the side.

Right: Deflect his knee to the ground.

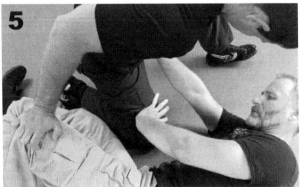

EXERCISE 61
PRESSURE-TESTING THE KNEE PIN

Place yourself on your back between two training partners. Have each partner take turns knee-pinning your torso. Allow the pin to dig in for a second at first and then escape at medium speed. The moment you escape, have the second partner pin you in succession. Continue without stop for a three-minute round. Escalate the drill to work at full speed, with your partners adding hits to distract you.

For solo work, lie on your back alongside a wall, holding a medicine ball on your stomach. Throw the ball straight up and let it land on your stomach. Be sure to keep your legs bent to help protect the groin. Try to absorb the impact fully with the stomach and only use the hands to guide and frame the ball. Be sure your tailbone is activated and your ribs are braced when absorbing the impact. Exhale on impact. After the impact, launch into a Russian bridge and turn to one side, toward the wall, and push the ball powerfully toward it. This will, in effect, push you away. Repeat this for two minutes and then switch sides.

Lying on the floor with your feet flat, hold the ball.

Throw the ball up in the air.

Lift up onto the balls of your feet.

For variation two, start in the Russian bridge.

Throw the ball.

Catch the ball and absorb the
impact by rolling onto your side.

THE MOUNTED POSITION

The mount is an extremely common street position that has been made even more common since the advent of MMA. It involves simply sitting on top of an attacker and offers terrific striking potential. While the mount is not an ideal street position to invest in because it leaves you vulnerable to multiple attackers, it is a nightmare when you find yourself in it.

Have your partner sit on you. Practice engaging a Russian bridge at medium speed. Pay attention to the simple reality that, when you bridge, your shoulders are on the ground and your hips are your highest point. This means that if your attacker is mounted higher, near your armpits, your bridge will have much less effect on you than if he were mounted lower and near the hips. Therefore, one level of work will be to push him as low as possible and to squirm yourself as high as possible.

EXERCISE 62
GROUND STRIKING

STEP 1: Have your partner mount you as high as possible so that his knees are directly under your armpits. With focus mitts or slaps, have him begin to throw hooks toward your head so that you can test your shields. Remember to invest in movement rather than trying to freeze on one spot. This means moving those shields as if you were washing your scalp. Even the slightest arm movement will help deflect shots. At the same time, rock from side to side, rolling alternating shoulders off the ground. When your partner is higher on your torso, the rocking action will be more difficult to generate in the shoulders, so focus on rocking the hips instead. In either situation, the key is to disrupt his base. This will create openings for your continued escape and will disrupt his precision when striking. As a general rule, do not rock fully onto your side, as this could allow the attacker to stop you there with his legs, making it easier for him to force you onto your stomach.

Step 1: Shield as your partner strikes.

STEP 2: Begin using that rocking motion to walk with your feet. As you switch from one side to the other, push away with your feet. This alone may start to move your attacker lower toward your hips. You will usually need to use your arms to facilitate moving him lower. To use your arm, post your bottom hand or elbow on his hips or thigh when you are on your corner. Keep your top hand high and shielding your head at all times. Your top hand can also be used to elbow downward into his groin or thigh, but these hits should only move a few inches and never low enough to expose your head. High repetition training is necessary to make this position familiar. You need to experience the breath inhibition, the pain, and even the panic in order to begin eroding it.

Step 2: Rock back and forth as you climb with your legs, pushing the attacker down onto your hips.

You can also practice striking from the bottom.

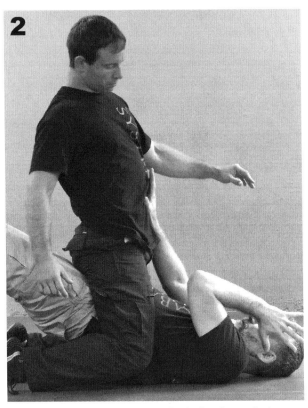

While bridging, rise onto the balls of your feet.

Keep your hips as high as possible
while rolling the attacker off you.

Finish with strikes from a dominant position.

SECTION
6

RESTRAINT TACTICS

You don't have to work very hard to get hypervigilant in today's world. The media's constant barrage reminds us that violence is all around us and promotes a natural tendency toward counter-aggression. In reality, however, the resolution of violence is far more complex. We cannot respond to every threat with equal force. There is a legal expectation to use only the degree that is necessary to end a threat. In today's increasingly litigious society, the pressure to respect these considerations is no longer exclusively the domain of the security or law enforcement professional. We are all vulnerable. Moreover, not every attacker will be a fearsome stranger. You may be called on to intervene among friends or family, or against smaller or less capable threats—all of which can increase the desire to have less-than-lethal options.

147

There are a lot of instructors out there who promote the idea that even attempting to restrain a motivated attacker is a needless risk, if not completely impossible. While I understand these comments are genuinely intended to help you protect yourself, I can attest that they are untrue. I have been called on to intervene numerous times against attackers who were much bigger, stronger, and more motivated. I was expected to contain outbreaks to protect clients and minimize property damage. It was often necessary to intervene against individuals who were smaller, female, or mentally ill. In the majority of these cases, it was possible to restrain the subject. Yes, responsible power and restraint tactics require more training. Yes, they place the defender at greater physical risk. But they also offer a lot of advantages:

- Restraint tactics, when correctly executed, reduce the likelihood of legal ramifications. If you have ever been snagged by the gears of the legal system after being involved in an altercation, you know full well the stress and grief this can bring.
- Effective restraint tactics reduce the potential for psychological damage. I realize that a lot of people don't even consider this. I know soldiers who have had to do some horrible things and are fully convinced they did what was necessary to protect their country. I know law enforcement officers who joke about the mandatory debriefings they were required to undergo after lethal-force encounters. I know hardened street fighters who discuss vicious acts of violence they committed without bravado or excitement, as calmly as if they were watering a houseplant. They may all be telling the truth. They may be particularly durable or well suited to such acts. Some may even be functional psychopaths. I also know people who have been debilitated by committing violent acts. I know many more who were not even aware of the subtle but continuous and cancerous changes that poisoned their personality.

The U.S. Defense Department has shown that domestic violence has risen in severity. We see this in statistical increases in frequency and severity of domestic violence committed by soldiers after they return from war, hyperexplosive acts like severe beatings, rape, and murder of family members. It is enough to simply accept that some very experienced, strong, and capable people are affected by committing violence and that, as humans, no one is immune, save perhaps the psychopath. I have personally experienced severe post-traumatic stress from a very justified and somewhat routine use of force. Moreover, the effects cropped up long after the initial event, even though far more violent encounters never affected me. Crossing the barrier of harming a fellow human being always carries a risk of psychological damage, regardless of the context.

- There is also what we might term a "social risk" of using violence. When I was a doorman, I quickly learned that the first person who needed to believe the force you used wasn't excessive was the one you were using it on. Excessive force could cause victims to come back with friends and weapons. More than one bouncer got curbstomped in retaliation during my time. Many others had to change clubs. About three weeks into my first job on the door, a group of large men came up and asked if I was a certain guy—I wasn't. They started to get heated. I was nervous, inexperienced, and working for a cheap owner who understaffed, so the only other bouncer on staff was on a break. The lead guy insisted I prove who I was and asked for my driver's license. Thinking that would solve it, I proved that I was a rookie and presented it. He looked at it, looked me over and said, "Thanks, Kevin," tucking my card in his pocket. "At least we know what you look like if we ever have problems with you." And then they walked away. That was a horrible feeling, and I wasn't even the guy who they were looking for! I found out later that night that my predecessor had changed clubs because he had beaten down a guy—a guy who obviously had friends.

The key component to remember throughout this section is that restraint tactics are an option. They are something we choose to use when we think they are viable and necessary. At any point, we must be ready to abandon them and disengage or escalate. In this section, I will outline a few of my go-to moves and illustrate the finer points I have picked up over the years.

THE HARNESS

When I started bouncing, there was no on-the-job training provided. Nor was there any standardization or certification. I was a skinny black belt in jujitsu who was far too small to be intimidating. At best, I looked like a malnourished junkie. I naturally got jobs that people with a more imposing appearance would not take. The only plus side—which I benefitted from years later, having survived it—is that there was a lot of action.

It took a few interventions to recognize that the "twisty-wristy" elements and flowery punch catches and traps did not happen. Clinching happened; biting and gouging happened. I became feral very quickly. I was getting my ass handed to me most nights. Had I not been partnered, I would have been hospitalized every night. I started cross-training in wrestling and judo, boxing, and muay Thai, and I started getting my ass handed to me in my training too, but very quickly it was happening less and less at work. In everything I did, I was clinching. I was chipping my teeth less, getting cut in the face less, and ending up on the ground less. I learned that working close and holding on let me be more effective and more protected. The very first intervention technique that began to emerge with consistency was the harness.

Simply put, when intervening from behind, shield your head as if you were washing your hair, flex the legs to lower your carriage a little, and charge in. Rather than try to reach for the face and neck, reach over one shoulder and under the opposite armpit. Clasp your hands together in front of the subject's chest so that your arms are diagonally around him like a seat belt. This will give you strong control of the shoulders to steer and help counter his striking effectiveness. It will also allow you to apply tremendous force to his trunk without putting his cervical spine or trachea at risk as you might if you simply pulled back on his throat. Keep your ear on his shoulder to protect your face.

To put your subject on the ground, lean him slightly onto one leg. Generally, it is easier to hook and pull with the top arm (i.e., if your right arm is high, step slightly to your left and lean left). This will either stumble the subject slightly, cause him to stretch his base or, more probably, create a single point of support (a density). Next, step deeply through the subject's baseline, striking him in the buttocks with your hip if possible. This will knock the subject's hips forward and force him to lean backward. Remember what we know about leverage and try to avoid pulling back forcefully on the shoulders as you drive forward with your hips. Instead, pull back on the shoulders and hang off them, and then lock that force in place as your fulcrum. This can be done as you are stumbling the attacker on his baseline. Then drive forward with your hips. This will help you avoid accidentally pulling his body into your face, will prevent you from losing your own structure, and will give you better control of your subject throughout the process.

Stay low and shielded as you enter from behind.

Step deeply through the subject's baseline.

Make sure that your giant step goes completely onto your heel and then rolls onto the flat of the foot.

5

Drive into the subject with your hips.

6

Step backward with your driving leg.

7

Finish by pulling your subject down into a sitting position.

EXERCISE 63
THE CRESCENT STEP

A great solo exercise for improving your explosiveness is to begin in your ready stance, rear heel loaded. Practice stepping forward with your rear leg as quickly as possible. Notice that if you step directly forward in line with your hip, your movement will tend to be slower. By contrast, if you step forward along a crescent path, first stepping in toward your lead foot and then exploding forward, you will have more power. Be sure to arrive in a loaded stance, with your new front foot firmly planted and your rear heel loaded. Also, when stepping through your partner's baseline, avoid landing on the ball of your foot. For the deepest penetration, seek to land on your heel first, rolling forward onto the arch and ball.

Start in a loaded stance.

Step forward with your rear leg toward your lead foot and continue forward on a crescent path.

Land with your opposite leg in front.

For additional solo ideas, practice performing the step while hugging a medicine ball or while carrying someone on your back. You can also pause at the junction step, when your rear foot is beside your front support foot, squat more deeply, and then practice jumping forward as far as possible as an exaggerated isolation for deeper conditioning.

Once you have buckled the subject's hips, you will be able to rest them on your lead leg if you wish. Depending on circumstance, you may choose to verbally de-escalate from there, adapt with standing restraints, or even transition to a choke. To continue putting the subject's hips to the ground, simply step back with your rear leg, sitting them directly on the floor. Some of the reasons the harness is so effective include:

- It is macro rather than micro. It allows you to latch on to something big and slow moving rather than trying to catch arms and fists midpunch.
- It protects you as the interventionist. When you harness someone, he will have difficulty hitting you with his arms and legs. He cannot headbutt you, and you can easily counter his attempts to throw you by simply hanging off him. The most he can do is slam you into a wall or drop you, and if you are working to actively stumble him and then intersect his baseline, he won't have the time. By comparison, intervening by grabbing his arm can allow him full access to counter hits with his legs and free arms and full counter-clinching potential.
- It works with the subject's natural movement, inviting him to forcefully sit down rather than trying to jam him forward onto his face. Even older, unfit individuals maintain the ability to sit and stand long after they lose the ability to sprawl.
- It protects the subject, avoiding impact with the throat in the grab and protecting his head throughout the struggle.
- It is scalable and always provides you with efficient, immediate options for force escalation when needed.

THE OPEN HARNESS

It isn't always possible to achieve a full harness. Some subjects will just be too large, and others may be able to bend forward so much or be so dynamic that you can't get the harness immediately. In these instances, you need to adapt your grip to an open harness.

To achieve an open harness, reach under your subject's armpit on one side in the same way. Instead of reaching across his body, simply reach up for his shoulder. Turn your thumb outward, with your palm toward the subject and

Bottom short hook.

Top short hook.

grab with a monkey hand, as high and deep above the deltoid as possible. With all five finger pads, pull and peel the deltoid forward to lock in the grip as if you were performing a one-handed pull-up. With your second hand, reach over your subject's shoulder on the opposite side. Your thumb should be pointed inward toward his neck and your palm downward toward the top of his shoulder. In exactly the same way, reach deep over his shoulder with a monkey hand and, with all five finger pads, pull back and down with your top hand. Again, you should be able to support much of your weight on that grip and even more using both hands simultaneously. From the open harness position, be sure to keep the side of your ear pressed against his back. Keep your elbows tight and pointing straight downward. All the mechanics for stepping through and back are identical to the closed harness.

EXERCISE 64
ADAPTING YOUR GRIPS

Working with a partner of roughly equal size, practice acquiring a closed harness and transitioning back and forth to an open harness. Isolate this for one three-minute round.

Next, have your subject slowly change positions, leaning from side to side and forward, to get used to adapting to these variables.

For the third round, have your subject wrestle at medium speed.

Begin in the harness.

Your opponent attempts to throw you over his shoulder.

Slide over his shoulder, landing on his side.

Slide your forearm across his face.

5

6

Steer his head in the opposite direction and force him to sit.

The Face Lock

Another option from the open harness is to seek a cross face lock. I recognize that this tactic is not permitted in all approaches and jurisdictions, as it is a spinal manipulation and carries a risk of paralysis and death. I include it as an option for escalation rather than as a primary consideration.

To perform a face lock correctly from an open harness, reach across your subject's face with your top hand. Turn your thumb toward the subject so that your palm is parallel with the ground and grind the first 3 inches of your wrist deeply into his face, beginning behind the ear and cutting across the cheek. As you apply this pressure, the subject will try to turn his body away to remain in line with his nose. Counter this by maintaining your underhook on the far side and keep your shoulder and chest firmly planted behind him, sandwiching him between your body and short hook. For added pressure, buckle the subject backwards and lean him on your thigh. Lean with your body, bending the crown of his head downward while maintaining the face lock.

The face lock.

THE CHOKE

There are two principal ways to choke a person unconscious: first by cutting off airflow and second by cutting off blood flow to the brain. We will refer to them as wind and blood chokes, respectively. There has been tremendous debate over the safety of chokes in recent decades with some law enforcement departments moving away from them and others prohibiting them entirely. In my opinion, this is unjustified. The only danger in chokes lies in a lack of proper training. I have used blood chokes repeatedly and consistently in live encounters and training. I have been choked to unconsciousness more times than I can remember (there is probably a brain damage joke in there) and have had no negative effects. Chokes are reliable, work in many situations, and are at the top of my list of essential moves. Air chokes are somewhat less reliable and do carry a higher degree of fracturing of the larynx or hyoid bone. They are also less likely to induce unconsciousness and are far less preferable.

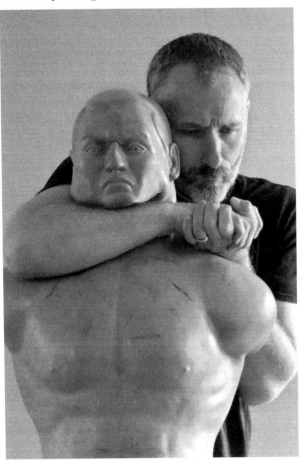

The air choke.

The blood choke.

EXERCISE 65
CULTIVATING THE PERFECT BLOOD CHOKE

To perform a blood choke correctly, slide your biceps alongside one side of your aggressor's neck, folding the arm so that the forearm is aligned on the opposite side. The arm should be bent in a V with your elbow underneath his chin. Achieve the blood choke by applying pressure inward to both carotid arteries. Many people rush to imitate variations of chokes that they have seen, most commonly the figure-four choke, where the arms are woven together and a hand is placed on the back of the head. The difficulty I have with this application is that people tend to prioritize pushing the head forward into the crux of the elbow, thus placing pressure on the trachea, which can be dangerous. Moreover, this muscle confusion robs you of efficiency. The difficulty is that in sport or casual sparring, an inefficient choke can cause more pain than blood impingement and so it can still earn you a tap. When it's used in a life-and-death situation, pain is less of a factor. People will endure and completely ignore high levels of pain. This forces you to apply more force, and since you are targeting the trachea to a large degree, this is a recipe for excessive-force issues.

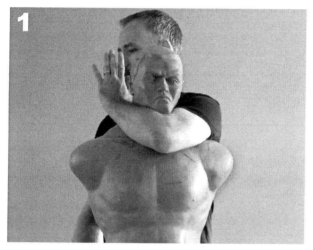

Force your wrist as hard as you can toward your shoulder, making sure your elbow is in line and under the subject's chin.

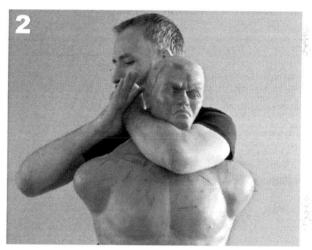

Add support to your wrist with your second hand.

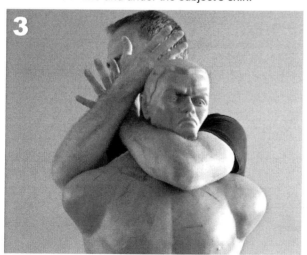

Maintaining pressure with your forearm, slide the support hand behind his head.

Grab as high on the arm and shoulder as you can and scissor the elbows inward.

I don't want you to have a blood choke that is good enough—I want it to be perfect. To achieve this, here are some deceptively simple exercises. These are easy and guaranteed to multiply the power of your choke against anyone. I urge you to incorporate them into your regular training.

STEP 1: In your solo training, practice making the shape of your basic V choke with one arm. Place your hand on your opposite shoulder. Notice that if you try to align your elbow with the center of your chest, your shoulder and back will get stretched and feel somewhat tense. If you simply let your humerus hang more naturally on your ribs or with the cradle of your elbow framing the edge of your chest, you will feel much more comfortable. This is an important first consideration in energy efficiency. When acquiring a choke, many people wage the fight where they find it and allow themselves to remain deformed or out of ideal alignment. By solo training yourself to contract where you are strongest, you are creating the habit of bringing the subject into your ideal alignment rather than volunteering for his. Train this simple action, comparing and contrasting center alignment versus corner alignment for three minutes. It is not enough for your brain to understand. You must give your body time to integrate this feeling.

In your continued training, an advanced variation can include holding a plank position on your elbow both in line with the center of your body and your shoulder. This is a far more extreme way to illustrate the point.

STEP 2: Begin squeezing the radial edge of your wrist (the thumb side) across your body toward the shoulder of the same arm. I refer to this as the "hitchhiker contraction" since I often illustrate it by extending my thumb. Using only your single arm, squeeze as hard as you can, as if you were trying to crush something between the radial bone of your forearm and your biceps. Try squeezing continuously for 30 seconds. A big part of this is teaching yourself to force hard while taking long, continuous breaths. Too often people hold their breath when applying chokes. This causes them to gas quickly and to continuously fidget with their hold, which constantly gives your subject the opportunity to partially recover. Practice squeezing in 30-second intervals for three minutes.

STEP 3: Anyone who lifts weights knows that a key to breaking through plateaus and expanding thresholds is to work with a partner to spot him. Now, we are effectively going to achieve the same result by spotting ourselves. Begin by squeezing your arm in the V choke, as outlined in step 2. Squeeze as hard as you can and sustain this for at least 10 seconds, maintaining maximum intensity. Next, slowly add the assistance of your free hand. Be sure not to clasp your hands together or to force against the edge of your hand, as this will encourage the wrist to buckle and the forearm to rotate, depriving your subject of the sharp cutting edge of your radial bone. Instead, push against the bones of your wrist. This will allow you to maintain perfect alignment and will prevent you from leaking power. Avoid going any lower than the wrist, as this will be "choking" your lever and deprive you of optimal mechanical advantage. You will notice that as hard as you may have been contracting with your single arm, the moment you provide even mild assistance from the second arm, there is a massive increase in perceived force. Here is the most important part: just like a spotter in weight lifting, you don't need to continue offering that support to be effective—you just need to help yourself get through the tough spot. Spot yourself by pushing on your wrist for a few seconds and then release it. You will notice your single arm is squeezing much more powerfully because you helped it get through.

This is an important exercise because it helps you recognize the capacity of each limb in sequence. Often, when people latch a two-handed choke of any type onto you, they compete with themselves, contracting the biceps and triceps of the choking arm simultaneously and then buttressing that with their second arm. They effectively create a static frame that is self-supporting around your neck to some degree rather than forcing constantly inward against the neck. The simple contraction-sequencing drill above is the most effective way I have used to bypass this muscle confusion in myself and thousands of students.

STEP 4: There are effective ways to choke with only one hand, as we will see shortly. Moreover, you could simply maintain pressure on your wrist with the second hand as detailed above, without releasing the spotting pressure for application. Still, the figure-four choke holds a prominent position in public consciousness due largely to its dominance in MMA. To apply and optimize your rear naked choke mechanics, begin exactly as prescribed in step 3. Your primary choking arm should be forcing powerfully, with your supporting arm assisting by pushing inward on the wrist bone. From that position, slowly slide the thumb of your support hand alongside your fingers without releasing any of the pressure so that you are exerting all your force through the heel of your support hand. Slowly slide the support hand behind the subject's head, keeping constant pressure on the primary chok-

ing hand, sliding the ulna bone across the wrist until you can touch your far shoulder with the support hand. In a rear naked choke, the hands are typically placed on the subject's head and the inside of the attacker's own elbow respectively. Instead, try to place each of your hands on your opposite shoulder so that your arms create an X. From that position, you may wish to close your hands into fists to protect the fingers from counterattacks. Slowly think of bringing your elbows together as if they wanted to touch. This will be a very subtle motion that will in effect scissor the subject's neck in your forearms.

Some people still argue that air chokes are good for shock value and inducing pain. Keep in mind that in sparring, people will rarely go for your eyes with full resolve or try to twist your testicle off or double you over and try to head-spear you into the wall. In the street, this is to be expected when you apply a choke.

Some colleagues have great success using wind chokes, and I have seen them in action. It is always dangerously close to catastrophe in my view. Early on, I prioritized wind chokes and had a severe injury in both the dojo and security settings that made me seriously reconsider my stance. Air chokes can be used for an instant to freeze the attacker for a blood choke with a greater degree of relative safety, but I would rather fake with a face lock or grind into the face for the same effect.

A correctly applied blood choke, by comparison, feels relatively safe and unthreatening to the subject for the first few seconds even though he is being weakened. By the time he realizes he should panic, he has already been significantly weakened. He feels tingles in the face and head, somehow off in his perceptions and, usually within about six seconds total, he is at a point of unconsciousness where he is no longer a threat. Once the subject is out, his posture will usually right itself and unfurl slowly. You will feel a sudden surge of his body weight. His eyes will usually stay open despite what is shown in films. His body will usually spasm or occasionally even go into a seizure. Do not panic. This is to be expected.

I once intervened on a guy who was shooting up in the hallway leading to the club's bathroom. He lunged at me during my interview phase. He hadn't noticed my colleague behind him who clamped a fast choke on him and smacked him into a cigarette vending machine. When the choke took him out, he went into the craziest seizure I have seen to date, and we just gave him some space to avoid the syringe until we were sure it was out of his hand. A client rounded the corner and said, "What happened?" My partner replied calmly, "Exorcism . . . the bathroom is closed." The expression on that patron's confused face as he backed up around the corner and the flailing junkie in front of him remain in my head as the worst reaction to a choke I have seen. Generally people just slump and make a small snoring noise.

EXERCISE 66
CHOKE RECOVERY

If you are going to train how to choke people, you need to train how to protect them after the fact. The safest blood choke in the world will be nullified if you drop your subject face first from standing height or roll him over into a puddle with his neck kinked. Begin with your partner in a standing choke. There is no need to apply real pressure to train this. Have your partner imitate resistance, reaching for your eyes, ears, hair, and groin. Ideally, buckle his hips just as you would in a harness takedown and lean on him on your lead thigh. Have the partner emulate unconsciousness after 6–8 seconds, suddenly going fully limp. You must train to be able to take his full and sudden weight shift. Slowly step back as you lower him to a seated position.

The first precaution is to release a few seconds after your subject goes limp. There is no need to continue choking. There is also no danger, providing you release soon after. If you remain latched on for 30 seconds or more, you now run the risk of causing brain damage. People often ask, "How will I know?" This is a normal and valid concern and a sign that you are training the right way. I guarantee you will know. The sudden increase in weight, and the shift from focused retaliation to even the most violent spasm, is quite different. As a precaution, however, train yourself to release slowly. This will give you better control of his body if he is unconscious and will also give you the option of reapplying the choke if he begins to fight back suddenly. As you release the choke, slide your support hand out and use it to pull back on your subject's forehead, pinning it against your chest so that it is pulling his chin up and opening his airway. Remove your primary choking arm, sliding it out and using it to securely cup a hand under his chin. Release the forehead and pivot to one side slightly, using the support hand to deliver a single, confident slap with a cupped hand to the base of the neck and brain stem, and then slowly begin to massage the nape. This will help to ensure that the arteries are open and feeding blood to the brain. Do not massage directly on the arteries as this may further impinge them. A strong pulling and kneading of the nape will stretch the tissue sufficiently on the sides of the neck and facilitate a quick resuscitation.

In situations where you may need to leave the subject to attend elsewhere, roll him onto one side in a standard first-aid recovery position. Fold the top leg over the bottom one so that the knee is high and bent with the foot locked behind the bottom knee. This will help prevent him from rolling over onto his stomach, where positional asphyxia may occur. Ensure that the chin is high so the airway is completely open. Tilt the mouth down toward the ground to facilitate drainage. There may be a lot of saliva coming out, and on a bad day even vomit. If you have time, fold the top arm and tuck it under the subject's head to help support it further, or stuff a jacket of something soft underneath to get the head back into correct alignment. You must train to do this until it becomes automatic and quick. Imagine being in a situation with family or friends. It escalates into violence. You are required to use a choke to full effect. As your first friend slips into unconsciousness, two others continue to tear each other apart. You must intervene again. You quickly drop your unconscious friend to the ground to assist the others. Without realizing it, he rolls onto his stomach, his arteries impinged and airway compressed. By the time the fight is over, it's too late. Your friend will have brain damage. This is the reality of not understanding how to help a subject safely recover.

After choking out a subject, gently support his head with both hands and lower it to the ground.

You may slide your subject's arm under his head for support and slide his top
leg onto the ground to prevent him from rolling onto his stomach.

 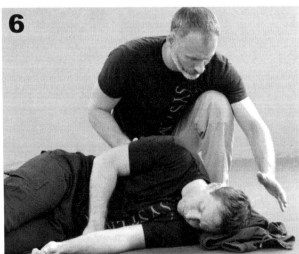

You may also use a folded jacket or similar prop to support the head.

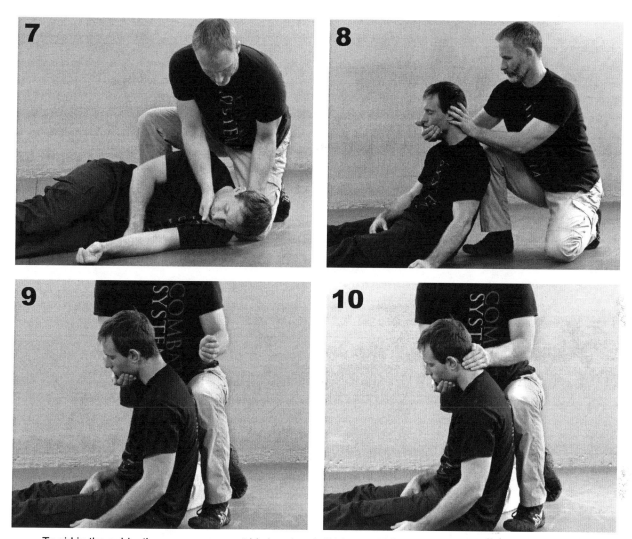

To aid in the subject's recovery, support his head and sit him up, while supporting his spine with your shin. Briskly deliver a single slap to the back of his neck while supporting his chin with your other hand.

THE MILITARY CHOKE

As mentioned above, there are extremely effective one-handed variations of the choke that can be performed. The most common is what we term a "military choke." Begin your blood choke in the standard V formation with your primary arm ensnaring the subject's neck, your elbow in line with his chin and your biceps and forearm clamping shut his carotid arteries. Rather than supporting your primary hand with your support hand, reach back behind your own head and grab your nape to close the choke. Note that if you remain in a palm grip, you will be contacting your subject's throat with the flatter surface of your forearm. For superior pressure, roll your grip on the ulnar (pinkie) edge of your forearm and make a fist, hooking your fist over your nape. This will provide a sharper edge and greater pressure. Under conditions of stress, it will be faster to first acquire the military choke with your palm and then to ratchet it tighter by transitioning to a fist hook.

The benefit of the military choke is that it leaves one hand free to work with weapons, restrain your subject's arm, or perform other tasks.

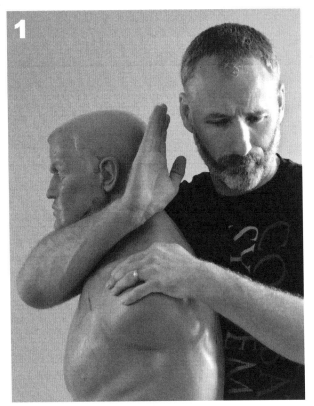

Acquiring the V choke.

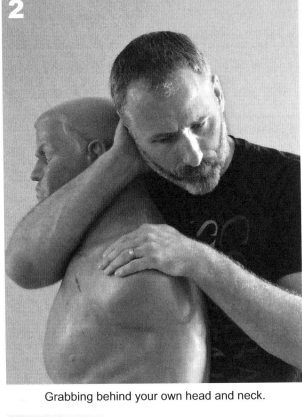

Grabbing behind your own head and neck.

The free arm can be used to wrap or trap the subject's arm.

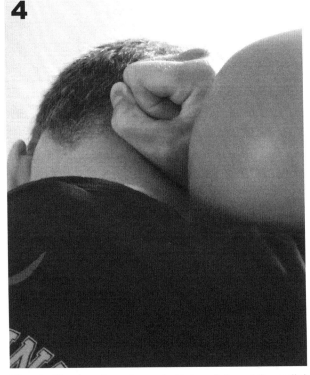

The choking hand can be curled into a fist, and the radial bone can be rolled to cut more deeply into the artery.

FRONTAL ENGAGEMENTS

The tactics that I have addressed thus far require access to the subject's rear diagonal flank. While circumstances may sometimes permit you to intervene directly from this angle, generally you will need to earn the position through hard work and effective tactics. Here are a few ideas for achieving control from the subject's front.

EXERCISE 67
THE SPIRAL TAKEDOWN

Engage your subject using finger whips or hammerfists to hack your way into an underhook and pike. This position is effective for restraining or walking a subject, but it is also a fantastic way to put him to the ground when accessing the harness is proving difficult. To drop an assailant, plunge his head down to the six o'clock position and raise his elbow to noon. A common error is to continue twisting the arm past this point, which will place you in a position of instability and will risk motivating the attacker to twist out and escape the hold. Instead, once you get to six o'clock and noon, plunge him directly to the ground with both hands. As you push the aggressor down, step around to his back. As your opponent falls, release contact with his head to avoid getting your arms crossed and tangled. Maintain contact with the underhook and slide your hand to the wrist of the aggressor, dropping one or both of your knees into his head and body on either side of his trapped arm. Stack your body and kneel your full weight into him as you pull upward on the body to keep it in a state of traction.

If resistance continues at this point, a very simple fight ender can be to bounce slightly on your knees to crush the rib cage or bounce the head off the ground. The spring provided by this can lift you back up to a full standing position to stomp on his head or ribs while maintaining control of the arm. Later, we will discuss control and restraint options.

Hack your attacker's lead arm down and away.

Snake into an underhook and
drive your lead forearm into his neck.

3

Maintaining control, plunge his head down to 6:00.

4

Step onto the far side of the subject's head.

5

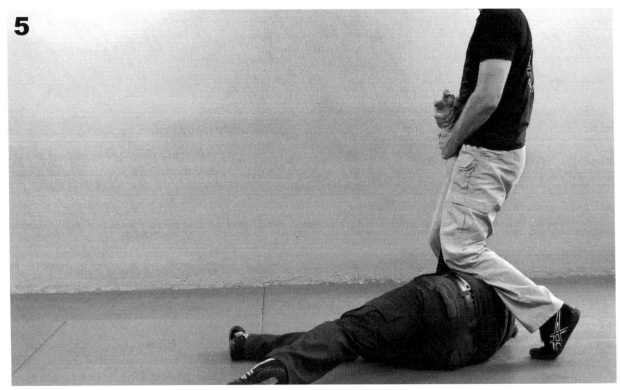

Drive him to the ground, maintaining control of his arm.

 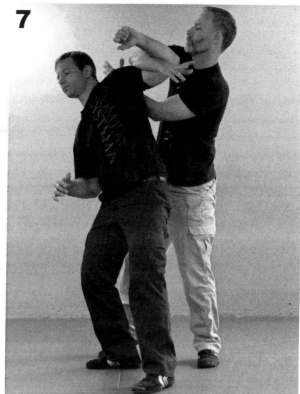

Be careful not to overtwist him, or he may spin out of the hold.

EXERCISE 68
THE SHOULDER VISE

When you have achieved the underhook and pike but are struggling to bend the attacker over, an effective strategy can be to switch your grip to a shoulder vise. To do this, lift your pike hand slightly and drop a short knife hand chop into your attacker's neck. Keep the blade of your hand in position as you reach up with your underhook hand and clasp your palms together. Do not interlock your fingers as that provides a weaker grip and fails to drive the ulnar blade of your arm into his joint. Keep your elbows tight and pull their shoulder joint into your sternum. From this position you can step back, pulling his shoulder forward and to the left as you take him down. Alternatively, you can lift your left elbow into his face to lever his head upward and put him down on his back.

From an underhook and neck frame, you may deliver short-range elbows and then hack your knife hand into the subject's neck.

4

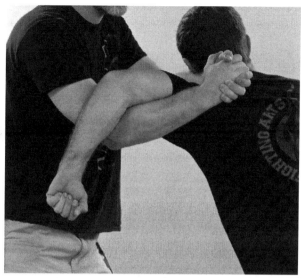

5

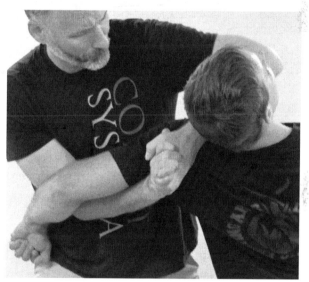

6

Top photos: Clasp your hands together driving the subject's shoulder downward.

Middle photos: Fixing your hands as your fulcrum, lever up into the subject's face with your elbow.

Bottom photo: Release your grip as the subject falls to avoid sacrificing your posture.

EXERCISE 69
TAKING THE BACK

If you achieve the underhook but feel that there is too much resistance to assert further control, another option is to slip through your subject's armpit to take his back. The key to achieving this is to begin with a tight underhook, pulling backwards powerfully with the pads of your fingers. Roll your hand over so that your pinkie is facing the sky and drive the radial bone near the wrist deeply into his shoulder and forward. This will naturally cause your elbow to flare upward, and this action can be amplified. Bend from the legs, plunging downward under the opening you have created, and slip to your opponent's back. I will detail a variety of options later in our treatment of restraint tactics. At this point, simple options include delivering a knee to the tailbone to push the attacker forward or driving a quick elbow into the base of the neck for a more severe effect.

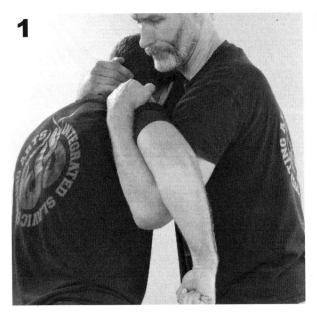

Begin in an underhand hook.

Turn your pinkie upward, raising your elbow to the armpit.

Change levels, plunging lower from your legs and slip under the arm.

5

6

7

Duck under the arm and take your subject's back, thus buckling him.

EXERCISE 70
ARM DRAG

From an outside Russian 2-on-1 arm tie, we have seen that you can jerk the subject down to his triangulation point and climb your second hand to his closer leg, far hip, lateral muscle, or neck. Entering farther from that point can be difficult. A common failure is to shoot in with the face and shoulder, keeping the hips back.

This allows the subject to adjust and square his body with yours before you can enter. To greatly improve your odds, lead with the shoulders but arch in with the hips, seeking to stick your hips into those of your partner. Stumbling the subject on his baseline will help unbalance him long enough to achieve this, as will hooking his closer leg with yours and hopping or pulling yourself in.

From an arm drag, jerk the subject down to his triangulation point.

You may climb up his body using his leg or hips to unbalance him.

GROUND CONTROL

Having felled your opponent, the next challenge is how to best maintain control of him. The first key principle is to make the subject carry your weight. There are four fundamental ground control positions you can find yourself in:

- Butterfly (standing knee pin)
- Three-point kneel
- Full kneel
- Full sprawl

Ideally, we would prefer to stay standing whenever possible, but control tactics generally require you to take a subject to the ground when he is resistant. To this end, staying as high up as possible is preferable, as it allows you the greatest mobility and the fastest disengagement should it be necessary. We will therefore begin with the butterfly pin.

THE BUTTERFLY PIN

The butterfly pin occurs when your subject has fallen onto his back and you have maintained control of his arm. It can be achieved naturally from either the spiral or harness takedown. From this position, walk toward your subject's ribs and wedge your shins in behind his head and side, respectively. Lifting with your legs, pull up on his arm. Ideally, roll the subject as much as possible onto his side and wedge your shins in farther to prevent him from rolling back off his side. Pinch your knees in together against the subject's arm (akin to a goalie stopping a puck in hockey) and stack your shoulders directly over your hips without leaning forward to maximize the distribution of your weight on the subject. Weight can be prioritized on either the ribs or the head or shared equally on both.

In the case of resistance, the smallest knee bounce on the subject can be devastating without any change in your position. Moreover, if the subject manages to roll onto his back, driv-

The butterfly pin.

ing your knees into his trunk and face can effectively keep him from rolling farther toward you. If you are unable to straighten the arm, counterpin the subject's arm against his body. If you are able to keep the subject on his side, switch to a figure-four arm lock and move north toward the head, as we will see in the following example. If the subject is able to roll completely toward you, kneel on the arm to delay it for a moment. Hack your hand that is closer to the subject's waist under the armpit of his far arm to achieve an underhook. Join your hands together in a shoulder vice and pull the subject toward you. To maintain control at this point, stand up slightly. Throw the leg that is closer to his waist backward for improved counterbalance and base and keep your other shin directly in his face. As you pull the subject toward you, he will be rolled onto his close side and effectively arrive in a face lock. Once you have pulled him up onto his side, maintain control in this position to talk him down, or else step back with your top leg and roll him fully onto his stomach.

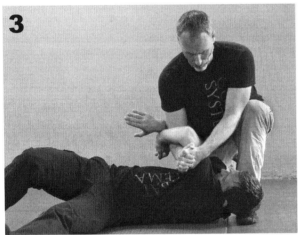

In the case of resistance, hack under the far arm, underhooking it,
and pull the subject by his arm, cranking his face against your shin.

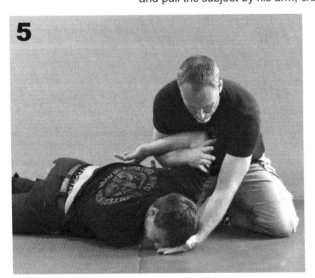

From here, you can steer the subject's face to guide him onto
his stomach and pin him with a shoulder lock and neck pin.

THE THREE-POINT KNEEL

In cases where the butterfly pin is not working or the subject moves before you can acquire it, the next alternative is to fall onto one knee. Let us assume you had attempted a butterfly pin on your subject's right arm but he retracted it and rolled in toward your legs. Move to your left, to a north-south position so that one foot is on either side of your subject's head and you are facing his body and feet. Drop your right knee

into his face, brushing through the cheek and driving his nose to the ground until you are firmly kneeling on the ground. Simultaneously thread your right arm into an underhook on his top (left) arm. The pressure you create on the subject's face will motivate him to turn onto his stomach, but the underhook will prevent him from doing so. There are numerous arm locks that can be applied from this position. This can also be used for cuffing or searching a suspect.

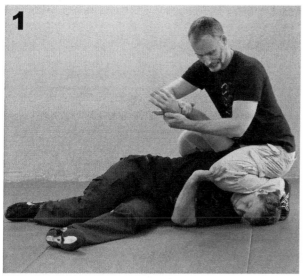

Place your shin on the subject's face . . .

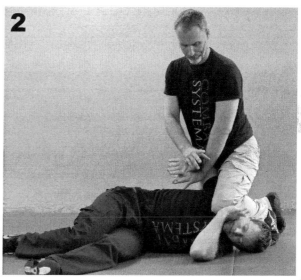

. . . and your knee on the ground
behind his back (three-point kneel).

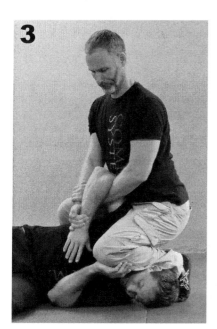

You have the option
to lock his arm . . .

. . . underhook the arm, protecting
your head behind his body . . .

. . . or squeeze his head
between your knees.

KNEELING POSITION

Often, you will be required to drop to both knees. From here, you can still exert tremendous control over the subject. Returning to the previous example, sometimes you may lose the subject's arm. In that case, drop onto both knees, sandwiching his head between your knees. For additional control, lean forward, posting your hands on his back or the ground, and pull with your knees to stretch out his neck. Any lateral pressure or rotational force applied to his neck will immediately cripple his capacity. Here are some options:

• **BASIC HEAD SCISSOR:** Think of your knees like blades in a pair of scissors. As you scissor his head, simply slide one shin back an inch toward the subject's temple. Keep your lower knee stable as a fulcrum. Push with the top knee inwards to bend the head to one side to achieve a neck crank.

Head scissor from a head squeeze.

Cross your ankles and stretch his head away from his body.

Twist your hips and his neck to the rear.

• **CROOKED HEAD SCISSOR:** From the same position, crisscross your ankles, balancing on the ball of the bottom foot. Squeeze your knees tightly together and pull the subject's head away from his body. Carefully and slowly pivot your hips and knees to one side, rotating the subject's face to the side and upward.

By scissoring one knee slightly past the other, you can achieve a painful crooked head scissor.

THE SPRAWL

In extreme cases, it will be necessary to drop to the ground completely in a sprawl. For maximum effect, explosively elongate your legs, dropping your hips into the subject. Anchor your legs on the balls of the feet or the inside edge of the big toes. This will give you more resistance and drive against the ground. If you imagine a "water line" delineating the vertical middle point of your subject's body, your goals should be to keep as much of your mass below that line as possible, to make getting rolled over unlikely, and to limit your subject's ability to turn on his side toward you. To maximize the effect of your sprawl, you can reduce the surface area that is in contact with the subject, transitioning from full contact with your torso to only the blades of your forearms to the points of your elbows. The points of the elbows in particular can be used to drive into the back alongside the spine to inhibit the ability of the lungs to breathe fully.

From a takedown attempt, pull your legs and hip back and backand away while steering the attacker's head to the ground and driving him into the ground.

An alternate view of the sprawl on the previous page.

EXERCISE 71
REVIEW VISUALIZATION

Imagine you are in a situation where you would prefer to not harm the subject, who could be a friend or family member. You engage in a clinch, snaking into an underhook and pike. Your subject resists, but you drive him along his baseline, stumbling him, and plunge him down, using a spiral takedown to put him to the ground. Before he can recover, you drop your knees in a butterfly pin and stretch out his arm. He refuses to comply and wrenches his arm free despite your best effort. You spin to a north-south position, dropping onto one knee in a three-point stance and steering his face to the ground. You underhook his arm to keep him from turning onto his stomach, but he is too strong. He rips his arm free, getting onto his stomach and back into alignment. You drop onto your second knee, sandwiching his head, but he gets his knees underneath his body and starts to drive into you powerfully. You explode your legs back into a sprawl and drop the full weight of your hips into his head and then spin to side control, maintaining your weight. You drive one forearm into the nape of his neck and your free elbow into his back and force him to carry your full weight. You can feel your feet sliding a little as you dig the balls of your feet more deeply into the ground. He stops for a moment, and you can hear him wheezing. He is finally getting tired. You maintain pressure, slowly reducing the point of your elbow to forearm pressure. You can feel his lungs expand underneath you. You continue talking to the subject, asking him to stop resisting. The subject whimpers, "OK, OK," and you circle his body back to the north position and return to a kneeling underhook control to allow him room to breathe while you continue to defuse the situation.

SECTION 7

WEAPON DEFENSES

One of the greatest dangers you can face is an armed opponent. Whether he only intends to intimidate you or is committed to hurting you, injury and death are always a very real part of the equation. The moment a weapon is present, every effort must be placed on avoiding conflict if at all possible. When situations cannot be avoided, you must enter resolutely using any tactic or level of force required to ensure your survival. In the following section, I will address some of the most essential weapon defense tactics.

STICK DEFENSE

THE UNIVERSAL ENTRY

We will begin our treatment of weapon defense by addressing the stick. The stick is the most primitive and readily available form of weapon on the planet. It comes in many forms: batons, baseball bats, broom handles, walking sticks, crowbars, and umbrellas. Sticks double the attacker's range and massively increase his speed and power.

The first principle of stick defense in Combat Systema is that you must either enter in directly and entirely into the attacker's space to invade the power-line of the weapon or maintain sufficient distance to keep away from it entirely. When facing a stick, it is absolutely essential that you remain in a loaded stance to maximize your mobility, responsiveness, and explosiveness.

A second key principle is that the stick can change trajectories rapidly. Attackers can hold the stick in a neutral position and effortlessly hit high or low without warning. Predicting the height of a stick attack can be extremely difficult, so we must brace for impact at all heights. Predicting the side from which the attack will come, however, is considerably easier.

When entering against a stick, the hands must be kept in a high shielded position to protect the head at all times. Lift the front leg so that the knee is as high as possible. Removing weight from the leg will protect it somewhat from impact while helping to protect the torso from impact. Launch yourself as far forward as possible off your back leg, plunging into the attacker's space, and latch onto him using any manner of clinch prescribed. We will discuss the specifics of contending with the stick in the clinch shortly.

As the shielded lunge becomes more comfortable, you should also train to switch your lead leg to meet attacks from the opposite side. While a universal entry can work, it is safer to study how to lunge off the rear leg, crescent-stepping during the lunge, to meet the stick with the outside of your thigh and shin whenever possible.

EXERCISE 72
THE SHIELDED LUNGE

Begin in a loaded stance with your hands held high in a ready stance. As you lunge forward, raise your lead leg as high as possible as you turn your hands inward into a high shielded stance. Land solidly, latching onto your attacker. Strive to lunge farther and farther with every attempt for three consecutive minutes.

For a second phase, begin in the same stance, practice leading with the rear leg, taking a lunging crescent step with the rear leg in toward your support leg and then exploding off and forward to land in an opposite lead. Be sure to keep your shields high at all times. Practice for three consecutive minutes.

For additional plyometric value, you may start in an exaggerated low stance, with the knees deeply bent. This will accelerate the conditioning of the legs.

Begin facing your attacker.

Shield with the arms and lead leg and explode inside the stick's power line.

Arrive with an instinctive clinch and immediately attack with rapid-fire knees.

EXERCISE 73
TAKEDOWN

After using your universal entry to enter against the stick, begin studying how to put the attacker down. Acquire and maintain control of the stick arm. This will usually occur by the use of an underhook or overwrap after entering, but it can evolve into baseball-bat grips and Russian 2-on-1 arm ties. Common options include:

• Stepping on the attacker's foot, or hooking or sweeping his leg while driving forward.

Step on your attacker's foot and push against his hip or kneecap to drive him to the ground.

- Using a spiral takedown from either the underhook or overwrap and pike.

Spiral the attacker's head underneath his overwrapped arm,
snaking your arm behind his head for control and driving strikes into him.

• Using basic hip throws to drop the assailant.

Drive the subject along his baseline, turn into him for a hip throw, and land in a butterfly knee pin while maintaining control of his arm.

In all these cases, seek to land in a butterfly knee pin while maintaining control of the arm.

STICK DISARMS

Many styles advocate complex fine motor disarms while standing. While not impossible, in my experience, there is very little time and control from a standing position. Moreover, there is very little protection provided to you as the defender. In Combat Systema, we generally advocate what we term "tree theory," which is the idea that when seeking to control an at-tacker, we prioritize treatment of the trunk first and the limbs second. Whenever possible, we seek to avoid fixating on small joint manipulations. Against the stick, this can be seen in our prioritization on putting the subject to the ground first. Once you have achieved a butterfly pin or similar control, much simpler options for disarms include:

• Grabbing the stick and stomping and grinding on the subject's inner wrist or hand to cause him to release the weapon.

Grab the stick and stomp the inner wrist to disarm your attacker.

- Grabbing the stick and kneeing on the inside or back of the subject's wrist while pushing the tip down and away from his grip to lever it out of his hand.

Kneel on the inner wrist and twist the stick over your thigh.

- Grabbing the stick and inserting your second forearm under the stick and then monkey-hand grabbing the subject's wrist to provide a fulcrum. Forcefully push down on the tip of the stick to strip the weapon.

Grab the stick, snake your free arm under the stick and over the attacker's wrist, and pry the stick away from his hand.

In every case, the stick is then available for you to use. Remember that armed assault falls into the highest tiers of use of force and generally justifies higher degrees of force to stop the threat.

EXERCISE 74
STOMP TRAINING

One great exercise is to have your partner wear two focus mitts. Lock up one arm as if he were holding a stick. Put him to the ground in your chosen manner. As the partner falls, have him position the mitt on his free hand firmly over his chest so that you can practice striking (emulating face and throat hits). Palms and hammerfist strikes tend to cause the most damage with the least risk to your striking tool. Next, slide your arm control up to the wrist and practice throwing it to the ground, stomping on the mitt as if you were performing a wrist disarm.

A second great drill is to simply throw a single focus mitt down on the ground within reach of a single step. Practice taking a large pivot step to land with a precise and powerful stomp on the mitt.

Have your partner hold two focus mitts.
Grab one arm as if it wielded a stick.

Put him to the ground

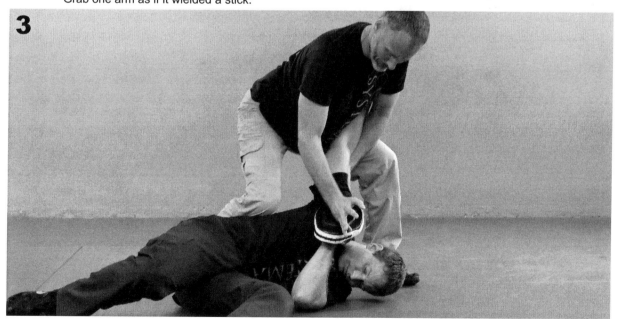

Strike the mitt on the chest, emulating head and throat strikes.

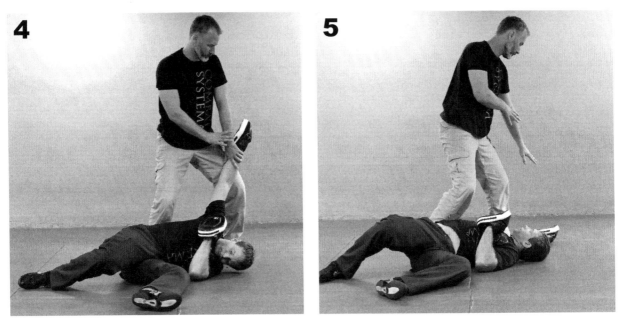

Control the second mitt as if it held the stick and throw it aggressively to the ground.

Stomp the mitt as if you were crushing the wrist or hand to disarm.

STICK CLINCHING

A key concept in Combat Systema is the idea of "educating the attack": constantly training to become a superior attacker so that we can improve our understanding of the threats we face and improve our defenses against them. In the domain of stick defense, one essential area to understand is the basics of stick clinching. Attackers who are proficient with the stick will intuitively use the stick to amplify their clinch. These commonly include turning the stick across either the nape of the neck or the back and gripping it with the second hand to pull forcefully in against the spine.

To counter this type of clinch, first ensure that your face is turned to the side, to protect your teeth and prevent your chin from being hooked and delayed on the attacker's shoulder. Maintaining control of the stick, use your free arm to drive into the space between you and the attacker. Ideal targets include the groin or pubis when your free arm is stuck low or into the throat when it is high. Rather than forcing entirely with your wedged arm, keep it firmly in place as a frame against the attacker and drive your hips back. This will help protect your structure and your balance. Knee strikes to the groin or inner thigh and grinding or spearing with the head or shoulders are fantastic ways to additionally disrupt your attacker. If the attacker still does not release his grip on one end of the stick to permit you to continue with your previous takedown, two immediate options for takedown within the clinch include:

- Step forward through the attacker's baseline while pushing forward until he falls backward. Step on his foot or hook his leg to assist the takedown. If the hold persists, you can easily land in a top mount position.
- Abandon arm control and transition to a bear trap with both hands, twisting the attacker to the ground.

After you enter against the stick, your attacker adapts, clinching with his stick.

3

4

To regain your structure, wedge your forearm into his neck, drive your hips back, and push his head away.

5

6

Load your free arm and powerfully cuff the back of his neck with your arm.

7

8

Using your free hand, drive the face back upward and twist his head back and around.

9

10

11

Once the attacker has fallen, grab a handful of his hair, driving his head into the ground, and stomp to finish the encounter.

CROSS-CHECK

Many attackers will opt to use a two-handed cross-check strike. In these cases, raise both hands to shield the impact, offering the more durable outer surface of your forearms. Try to absorb the impact with your legs and a slight upward ramping motion. Immediately turn your palms outward and drop them down to catch the stick with both hands. Drive the stick down low to hip height to be out of your way and spear up with your head. Follow up with a cutting elbow to the face and then continue with the control or finish you prefer.

The attacker prepares to strike with a two-handed cross-check.

Greet the stick with the more durable outer forearm and screw the palms outward and downward, grabbing and driving the stick down as you strike with a head spear to his face.

ZIGZAG ENTRY

As you become more comfortable with stick attacks, increase the training distance to a farther preengagement distance. At this distance, you can incorporate a larger focus on preemptive evasion, baiting the attack, and absorbing impact when generating the power to traverse the distance between you.

If you are in a left-leg lead and the aggressor is attacking from your left but you are still outside his striking range, rather than waiting for him to advance, you can preemptively take an additional step forward with the rear leg. Explode inward with the right rear leg and crescent-lunge outward toward the inside of the attacker's striking range. The goal is to step as far across his swing path as possible. This will bait him to swing across his own body, where his range of motion is less comfortable and his balance is compromised, giving you more reaction time than if you had entered in a straight line. Immediately bounce off that step, taking a second crescent lunge with your left leg advancing toward the left, impacting with your attacker. You will have effectively taken two quick steps in a zigzag pattern, to the right and then the left, lunging powerfully forward.

When you have a larger distance to cross, step forward, away from the stick first, and then spring forward with the opposite leg and drive into your attacker.

KNIFE DEFENSE

It has been commonly stated that a major advantage of a knife is that it never jams or runs out of ammo. A single stab or slice can affect numerous body systems, draining you of strength, focus, and endurance. Efficiency can erode at lighting speed after contact with a blade. Knives can also come in a variety of forms, including everything from screwdrivers, broken bottles, box cutters, and kitchen cutlery. Even the smallest blade can be lethal. It cannot be stressed enough that whenever possible, conflict should always be avoided. This is massively amplified when a blade is present. If you detect a blade, do everything you can to de-escalate or avoid the conflict whenever possible. If you must engage, use everything in your surroundings to your assistance, moving into doorways or near columns to limit the attacker's access to you, and use anything that you can as a weapon. We will discuss this in more depth in our treatment of improvised weapons.

The first step in blade training is to understand movement potential. Back in our discussion of plasticity, I outlined a simple push versus yield drill in exercise 6 that showed you how to improve your body intelligence and adaptability. In Combat Systema, we generally introduce blade and firearm training in the same manner—beginning with slow, exaggerated contact and teaching the body how to yield to pressure. This training methodology is one of the most misunderstood aspects of the Russian martial arts, yet I am including it because I believe, and have consistently found, that it is also one of the most unique and advantageous.

The key principle is that fear and tension rob us of efficiency. All attacks carry the potential of triggering fears, but knife and gun attacks in particular tend to be more foreign to most practitioners. As a result, when threatened, they indulge their most primal and basic reflexes rather than apply any specific tactics. In his book *Deep Survival*, author Laurence Gonzales stresses that reflex is not necessarily the best response in a given situation. Rather, it is simply the response that has generally worked the best for the majority of the species in the majority of situations.

EXERCISE 75
YIELDING TO STABS

Have your partner firmly hold a training knife in either an orthodox or icepick grip. Allow him to slowly and deeply begin to stab your body. It is essential that you work slowly enough to allow your body to authentically respond to the pressure that is being provided. Do not try to anticipate or guess what your partner is going to do. The goal of the exercise is to feel where the pressure is coming from. We all have physical limitations in our mobility. Some of them are biomechanical, but many are made worse by tension, fear, and a lack of familiarity with our bodies. A good way to approach this exercise is to remember that it is in no way a combat application—it is purely a biomechanical exploration and physical conditioning exercise. During this exercise, you are at the mercy of your partner and the challenge is to respond entirely to his lead. For the purposes of this exercise, it is impossible to respond too late to the stimuli provided by the knife—it is only possible to respond too soon. Relax and respond without judgment.

- For the first three-minute round, have your partner limit his attacks to slow straight stabs.
- For the second three-minute round, limit the attacks to slashes, again slowly and deeply.
- For the third three-minute round, integrate both types of attacks.

In all cases, respond entirely with your body. Do not use your arms in any way to deflect or assist.

In the case of direct stabs, yield to the direct pressure of the knife's tip.

Against slashes, move with the slice to reduce friction and allow the knife to pass along its original trajectory.

ADDING DEFLECTIONS

The next step is to begin integrating your arms. As we saw in our treatment of hand-to-hand work, we start with the worst-case scenario so that we can prioritize proximal learning and then evolve to distal movements with the limbs. Like a matador, we seek to escape the line of force first and use the evasion to create our deflections and counterattacks. When working against the weapon, begin with the previous exercise, feeling the stab or slash deeply in your body. You will notice the arms naturally want to move away from the body as counterbalance. The key is to permit the arms to contact the stabbing arm without adding resistance or overreaching. Simply use them to create a frame.

For the first phase of training, allow contact with the body and let the contact move you. You will in effect be deflecting too late. Progressively evolve to preemptive evasion with the body. This should seem as if the body melts away from the point of the impact and the arms serve as a natural ramp, off of which the stab slides.

EXERCISE 76
ISOLATING DEFLECTIONS

For the first three-minute round, isolate stabs and slashes to the stomach and groin, and maintain your arms in a lower-frame position. Your arm should swing naturally like an elephant's trunk and seek to deflect only enough to clear the weapon. Avoid batting the knife away with force—it would only add power to any incidental cuts that may occur during the deflection. Instead, keep the knife close.

From a lower-frame position, evade with the trunk and gently swing the arm to help create distance.

For your second three-minute round, isolate stabs to the chest and plexus versus middle- and lower-frame deflections. Rather than flapping your elbows directly up and down like a chicken, think of originating the movement in the head of the shoulder, rolling the shoulder up toward the ear and either forward or backward depending on how you are deflecting. This will produce a more elliptical motion that is both more efficient and continuous.

Against mid-height attacks, use the elbow like a wing to redirect the weapon safely away and guide it along its original trajectory, adhering to the weapon arm throughout.

1

2

For the third three-minute phase, work stabs and slashes to the face and throat. From this position, you can use deflections that employ the shoulder from a lower-frame position, the arms and facets of the arm and elbow in a middle frame, or the forearms and elbows in an upper frame. Again, feel the movement beginning in the torso and the shoulder rather than only working from one aspect of the arm stiffly. The arms should move naturally and continuously and stay close to the body as if they were washing the body and head.

When approaching knife defense, there is always a huge combination of fear and excitement. Students want to feel safe immediately. They want to show what they know or end the threat quickly, and in doing so they generally overreact or impale themselves to some degree. With the knife, more so than anything else, less is more. Prioritizing evasions and deflecting close to the body will let you get in close enough to the wielder to effectively counter him. Slow things down. Allow yourself to see how you are reacting, what triggers your flinch, and where your body is limited, and resolve these weaknesses from the beginning rather than insulating them with more fear.

3

Against high-line attacks, meet the weapon hand with your frame and blend with the force.

Another option is to twist from the body and redirect the knife on a straight path with an arm screw.

USE OF THE FOREARMS

Whenever possible, we seek to prioritize contact with the outer forearms as we discussed in our earlier treatment of shielding. The inner forearms are more vulnerable and rich with arteries, veins, and tendons. Cuts to the inner forearms are generally far more damaging than cuts to the outside. Moreover, the dominant flinch response in our arms and hands is the grasp reflex—the desire to reach for and grab when surprised. We see this most clearly when someone is falling. The identical response gets triggered when you are blitzed with a knife. People reach desperately for the threat in an attempt to neutralize and to some extent identify it. At a rudimentary level, this is certainly helpful and better than no reflex at all, but when we have a fraction of a second more awareness and preparation, we would far prefer to not needlessly endanger ourselves.

EXERCISE 77
OUTER FOREARM THEORY

An effective drill for isolating the use of the outer forearms is to have a partner begin slowly and continuously stab and slash you with a training knife. For optimal isolation, have the attacker assume a fixed stance, without footwork. To begin, you should also remain static but with your feet as close together as possible. Because this position is less familiar and comfortable than a standard stance, students will tend to forget about their bodies less. They will be forced to deeply feel bodily evasions as they compensate with deep flexions in the knees and rotation of the torso. For the first three-minute round, your goal is to always evade from the body first, all the while keeping contact between the attacker's weapon arm and your outer forearm, as if they were attached to each other by a pivot. The aggressor should prioritize attacking the trunk and face only with slow to medium speed and force. The defender should seek to adhere with a single arm, switching smoothly to the free arm whenever it feels necessary rather than at a fixed number of repetitions.

The second three-minute round should evolve to include the attacker also being able to hook and slice the arms themselves, particularly on the return from attacks to the body. You will now be required to screw the arm and to deeply recruit all the joints of the arm to escape.

For the third round, you stand more comfortably with the feet shoulder-width but the body still square to the attacker. Allow the attacker to take a single step in any direction to increase his mobility and to include cuts to the legs. You should continue to use your outer forearms to deflect, but you may now also move your legs, screwing the legs and pivoting on your support foot to prioritize contact on the less arterial outer thigh and buttocks and protecting the vulnerable inner thigh and groin. Care should be taken to avoid bending forward and jeopardizing the face. Instead your arms should protect the head and body and the legs should protect themselves. Emphasis should be placed on flexing with the knees and plunging downward with the body rather than leaning forward.

1

·The attacker targets your lead leg.

2

Pull your leg away, greeting the weapon arm with the outside of your lead forearm.

Adhere to the weapon arm as you reposition your leg and deflect the weapon.

Remain stuck to the weapon arm with the outer forearm driving the weapon away and setting you up to counterattack.

THE "X" AXIS

One specific notion that begs mentioning here is the role of the axes of the shoulder and the hips. Take a moment to consider the basic act of walking. As humans, when we walk, we swing our arms in the opposite direction of our legs. When we place our left foot forward, we swing our left arm backward. As we discussed at the outset of the book, the spine is the engine of movement. A human without legs is able to create rotational movement in the hips to move forward. This same motion is what motivates our legs to move. Arm motion creates an angular momentum that counterbalances this rotational movement and gives us stability when we move. Current research suggests that arm movement is passive at slow speeds, with the arms simply swinging like pendulums from the shoulders. Again we see proximal to distal movement in action. At higher speeds, the arms appear to move with active contraction, and a great deal of sport performance science has been dedicated to refining the swing—for example, considering the specific hand position or angle of the forearm in sprinters.

When most people approach fighting, however, they unintentionally stifle the natural power of this "X" axis. They protect themselves through the efficient proxemics of blading, zoning, and fencing, but often inadvertently limit their range of motion as they close up their bodies and tighten their muscles.

A good first step to unlocking the power of the "X" axis is to begin in your fighting stance, hands high and open, rear heel loaded. From a static position, elongate your lead arm to your maximum capacity. Ideally, measure the length of your reach to have a reference point. Also note your sense of balance at full extension. Next, elongate your rear hand, twisting deeply from the hips without leaning forward. First, you will notice it is much more stable. As noted above, asymmetric arm sway balances the rotation of the spine. Most people are surprised to realize that as a by-product of this stability, they actually have better reach with the rear hand. Naturally, because the rear hand has more distance to create power and more spinal torque behind it, it is capable of delivering much stronger hits.

EXERCISE 78
THE TWISTED LEAD

One great way to recruit the power of the "X" axis in your combative arsenal is to employ a twisted lead. In a conventional combative stance, the lead shoulder and leg are on the same side (i.e., if you have your left leg forward, your left shoulder will be in front). In a twisted lead, the opposite is true (i.e., when you have your left leg forward, your torso is twisted so that your right shoulder is slightly in front of your left). It must be stressed that initially this can seem quite awkward. Moreover, this is not a stance but rather an aspect of movement, which we will isolate here to improve its capacity.

In phase one, adopt your conventional stance. Practice reaching slowly in the air with your lead side as if firing off slow-motion finger whips. Now twist your rear side shoulder forward until it surpasses the former front shoulder. Practice launching finger whips from the rear side lead and returning to a twisted lead rather than your conventional stance. You will notice that the twisted lead is not generally your maximum possible rotation. You will generally still maintain the capacity to elongate a little further for a twisted lead jab or finger whip.

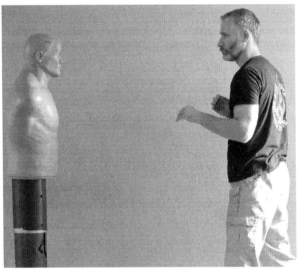

Orthodox lead.

Shorter reach.

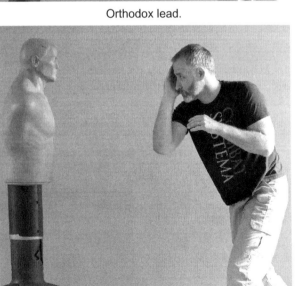

Twisted lead.

Longer reach.

In phase two, return to a conventional stance. Have a partner extend a swing or stab with a training knife to the outside of your orthodox lead (if your left leg is forward, have him swing toward your left side and freeze the swing in the air). Study the different ways you could contact the static swing with your left-side frames and deflections. Now, twist into a twisted lead and practice contacting with your rear-side arm. You will notice that the twisted lead provides you with strong reach and capacity even with the rear arm. Perhaps even more important, when you reached with your lead side, there was no movement required in your torso. When you employed the twisted lead, you began to turn your side away from the weapon.

Isolating the twisted lead allows you to explore evasion from the trunk without necessarily moving the legs. It also maximizes the role of the rear hand and allows you to share blocking and counterstriking responsibilities with both arms. For a third phase of work, play freely against slow- to medium-speed attacks. Evade and deflect all heights and zones of attack. During your movement, practice isolating an orthodox fighting stance, where the lead shoulder and leg are on the same side, and then switch for a number of reps to the twisted lead. You will notice it unlocks new movement potential and options.

In the end, the twisted lead should occur for an instant. It is an aspect of continuous movement and not a magical stance to be adhered to in all circumstances. Sometimes it can be used to load the body for unorthodox strikes and rear-hand leads or to bait the attacker. Ultimately, it must be a component of your total movement arsenal, which includes footwork.

ZONING

The next component of knife defense to consider is the role of zoning. We have already seen how zoning can preemptively improve our survival statistics by preloading our body to one side of the attacker to improve our odds. Now we will discuss the role of zoning during dynamic movement.

In a conventional boxing dynamic, generally we prioritize learning how to "circle out" and move away from the power hand of the opponent. If we are boxing someone with his left hand forward, we shuffle and slip to our right to maximize the distance between his hand and our head to give us optimal reaction time. When zoning to the outside, we can safely step back on a diagonal, laterally to the side, or forward. All movement will be difficult for the attacker to reach and will require him to twist awkwardly or reset his footing. Next, students are taught how to circle inward toward the power hand of the attacker. When circling in, we seek to avoid the ideal striking distance (roughly arm's length). We, therefore, seek to either smother the rear hand to rob it of its power by stepping in, or else step in and as far away as possible from in and away, as far away as possible from the power hand to bait the attacker to swing for us, opening himself up for counterattacks.

EXERCISE 79
REVISITING THE JUNKYARD DOG DRILL

Have your partner stand with his rear heel touching the wall, as you did in Exercise 11. For the first phase of the drill, have your partner isolate lead-hand knife attacks. Since your partner is committed to the wall, you can freely move in and out and better gauge your distance with safety. Begin by studying your capacity to first slip diagonally away from the swings for a three-minute round. This can be done simply by leaning back with the torso but will usually require a small step back on the angle.

For the second round, study your ability to move laterally to the outside of the jabs. This can be done simply by slipping laterally with the head and shoulder without taking a step, or by taking a small V step forward with the rear leg.

For the third phase, study your capacity to enter on the outside of your partner's stab. This will require slipping with the head first and taking a large V step with the rear leg. The slip and step should occur in immediate succession at a rhythm that matches the very fastest speed with which you clap your hands.

For the fourth round, study your capacity to step to the inside of the jab. Begin with stepping in and smothering the power hand. At minimum, this should include keeping your shields high to protect yourself. The simplest counter-attack from a shielded position is to drive inward with the points of your elbows, spiking the attacker in the face, throat, and chest. As your comfort grows, you may also wish to check the rear hand with the palm to pin it to the torso, delaying it long enough to deliver strikes with your rear hand.

For the fifth round, isolate slipping to the inside, away from the partner's reach. Step inward as deeply as possible. Have your partner reach for you with his rear hand to test the safety of your distance. Study your capacity to intercept his reach with low-line kicks slowly and calmly. Progressing too quickly will only reinforce any existing weaknesses in your movement.

The ability to move to the inside and outside of your aggressor is essential. In boxing, it is possible to dominate your strategy by circling outward and to circle inward as an exception to break your rhythm. Boxers and strikers are far less likely to switch leads and even less likely to maintain efficiency if they do so. A knife wielder, however, can freely change his lead, bringing the knife forward or back, even changing hands without much loss of capacity. Constantly circling outward against a knife can too easily allow the attacker to time your movement. Consider the jab in boxing. When two boxers engage, the jab lands repeatedly. Were that fist replaced by a blade, every touch would be seriously injurious.

Round one: Begin by practicing movement outside the weapon's range.

Round two: Evolve to moving laterally along the perimeter.

3

Round three: Next train yourself to step forward.

4

Round four: Practice shielding and moving inside the arm's range.

5

Round five: Practice moving inside the weapon's arc, far enough away to remain out of range, and draw the attacker to you.

EXERCISE 80
THE BUTTERFLY STEP

Equip your partner with a training knife. I strongly suggest wearing protective goggles or a helmet with a visor and working with a flexible training knife to reduce the risk of injuries. Begin moving at a slow pace. For this drill, the knife attacker can step, lunge, and move freely. In your defense, practice varying your movement, circling outward to all depths. Practice breaking your rhythm frequently, moving away from the blade to the inside to bait the attacker and draw his attack away from his body. For the first phase, prioritize avoiding contact, deflecting only when absolutely necessary. Allowing yourself to neither enter nor neutralize the weapon is an exhausting but important isolation. It will bring you to a point where you are surprised and continuously forced to adapt. For the second phase, integrate counterattacks.

This type of footwork is often referred to as "butterfly stepping" since it resembles the erratic pattern of a butterfly's flight, as you are constantly stepping in new directions.

PSYCHOLOGICAL DELIVERY MECHANISMS FOR KNIFE FIGHTING

When considering our combative capacities, all aspects of training can be classified as either:

- **TOOLS:** The specific grabs, strikes, or techniques in our arsenal.
- **ATTRIBUTES:** Our specific capacities and characteristic—e.g., age, size, height, strength, speed.
- **PHYSICAL DELIVERY SYSTEMS:** This encompasses our ability to move—e.g., flexibility, footwork, rhythm.
- **PSYCHOLOGICAL DELIVERY SYSTEMS:** This refers to all the behavioral components of our arsenal that can justify why we are moving or acting the way we are. This includes feigning weakness, cooperating, acting calmly, gesturing, using verbal tactics, and making or avoiding eye contact.

When we are confronted with a knife, for example, in a mugging or hostage situation, most styles simply address physical techniques for addressing the knife hand. What is infinitely more important, in my experience, is what you do before your technique. Most practitioners simply launch their technique from wherever they are. Some even volunteer to worsen their position, lowering their hands in nervous anticipation like a gun fighter from the Old West. Others even raise their hands with manifest aggression. The odds are already stacked against us when we face an armed attacker. We must do everything possible to reclaim any advantage we can.

EXERCISE 81
JUSTIFYING YOUR ACTIONS

Always begin by attempting to blade, zone, fence, and load your stance. If we simply do this unthinkingly, however, we run the risk of being obvious and triggering an attack. We must justify our actions. Imagine a knife-wielding attacker standing in front of you. He has surprised you, pressing a knife into your face. You can see the blade clearly out of the corner of your eye, and you can feel the cold steel on your cheek. The stranger is demanding your wallet. As he shakes and shoves you, you take a small step, feign a stumble, both zoning and loading your stance as you slowly raise your open hands in a show of submission, saying: "OK, OK, whatever you say." You have begun to engage him, which has already improved your defensibility without triggering any alarms. In fact, you are showing him respect and understanding, and cooperating with his demands.

"Listen, my wallet is in my front left pants pocket," you say, maintaining eye contact. You softly and slowly point down to your pocket and seem to offer your hip slightly. You glance down at your pocket for a second and then back up and say, "I'm going to take it out of my pocket—do you want me to put it on the ground or give it to you in your hand?" The moment he pauses to consider your question, you latch onto his neck and rocket forward with a knee to the groin. He gasps almost to the point of vomiting. You drill another knee into his throat and then his face as he buckles and falls limp.

The attacker holds you at knifepoint.

As you deescalate, direct
his attention to the wallet in your pocket.

During this moment, ambush him with a strike to the throat and
follow quickly with a knee to the groin and a finishing strike to the head.

FINISHING

In keeping with everything that we have seen so far, you don't want to fixate on the blade. While neutralizing the blade is definitely prefer- able, continuing to focus only on the weapon and wrestling for ownership will get you killed. Fight the wielder, not the weapon. The following exer- cise is a great way to break this habit.

EXERCISE 82
STATUE ATTACKER DRILL

Have the aggressor hold his training knife in any position, from stance to frozen swing. Oriented on the outside of his body, begin with your arms or hands contacting the body in various manners. Without sacrificing control of the weapon, study how you can put the attacker to the ground using the principles of structure breaking described earlier. As the subject falls, maintain control of his arm, seeking a butterfly pin as described in our treatment of restraint tactics. Keep it simple: knee drops and stomps to the head and body in rapid succession are easy and extremely destructive. They will often cause the attacker to relinquish his hold of the knife. You may also knee into the triceps or drop your shin on the elbow to destroy the joint.

After a round of isolation, repeat the exercise, beginning on the inside of the attacker's frozen posture. You may wish to put him down directly from this position or else pass the weapon to acquire his outside, by driving it into the attacker and then circling outside.

Your partner holds the knife out at arm's length.

Practice moving inward and deflecting the weapon arm, flowing directly into a fluid takedown and driving your aggressor to the ground.

Control your aggressor on the ground, guiding his arm into a stomp destruction to finish.

ESSENTIAL TECHNIQUE

One of my favorite techniques for catching circular swings and stabs to the body is to keep my close arm in a low frame, slightly ramped away from my body to clear the blade. Using a twisted lead, I cross-check with my free arm, driving the weapon low and then into the subject's body, as I circle out. Riding the attacker's natural desire to stab again, I guide the weapon into an elbow grab and then complete the Russian 2-on-1 as I head-spear the aggressor along his baseline.

1

The attacker swings at your ribs; keep the close arm in a low ramping frame away from the body.

2

Twist your body to escape the incoming force and greet the blade arm with the outside of the far arm.

3

4a

Deflect the arm into his body and pass it to the opposite side, catching it in a Russian 2 on 1.

4b

View from the opposite side.

In the case of straight stabs, an inward lower-frame deflection can arrive directly in the 2-on-1 and be completed in the same manner.

When strikes drift higher, the same tactic can be used to jam the swing and acquire an underhook and pike.

As another option with the twisted lead, greet the attacker with a blended frame.

Propeller your lower-frame arm into an underhook, clasp your hands together, and acquire control of their arm by driving your radial bone into the muscles of the attacker.

Raise his arm while plunging his head downward and drive him into the ground while controlling his knife arm.

GUN DEFENSE

Firearms are becoming an increasingly probable threat in our daily lives, particularly in North America. Much of what we have seen regarding knife defense and empty-handed tactics will apply here directly so we will use this opportunity to review some concepts and to introduce some new specifics.

EXERCISE 83
EVADING THE LINE OF FIRE

When beginning gun defense, the most common first step in Combat Systema is to return to the push and yield drill we saw against the knife and with empty hands. Naturally, no one is likely to push with a gun. Rather, the purpose of the drill is to increase body awareness for yielding. This is not a direct application. In learning to yield when your partner pushes with a gun, you are reinforcing a bodily understanding of the weapon's line of fire. What becomes more important here than even in knife work is that when you evade the weapon, you evade its path completely. Individuals will often only move their body, keeping their arms frozen and vulnerable to attack.

For the first phase of the drill, simply focus on evading the line of fire. Feel free to stop and analyze your movement at any time and have

your partner help you by indicating if he sees you have failed to clear the line.

For the second round of this drill, allow the evasion to create countermovement in your arms. Rather than simply deflecting the gun, study how you are able to secure it. Here are two helpful guidelines when securing the weapon:

- Keep your grabs direct and efficient. When you move your arms, think of Leonardo DaVinci's Vitruvian Man. The alignment of your hands is directly relative to the position of your arms. When your hands are above elbow height, they will tend to have the fingers pointing upward. Therefore, when grabbing gun threats at the height of your solar plexus or higher, your thumbs should be on the bottom of the grip. When your hands are below elbow height, your fingers will begin pointing downward. Therefore, when contending with gun threats below the plexus, your thumbs will tend to be on top of the grip. This may seem self-evident, but I often see people cramping their wrists into awkward positions when trying to grab the weapon, which robs them of speed and power.
- A second helpful rule is to anchor your elbows against your body. Once you have latched on to the weapon, compress your el-

In phase one, exaggerate your understanding of line of fire by having your partner push you with the barrel of a training gun.

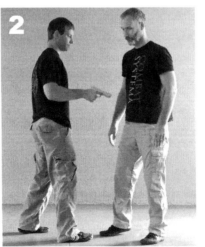

After each push, have him retract the gun and push in a different direction to a new body part.

Always be sure to completely clear the line of fire through efficient body movement and evasion.

bows in tightly toward your trunk. This will give you the support to better resist pushes from the gun wielder.

For the second phase, evade in the same manner.

Use the evasion to create the deflection. Make sure that all body parts completely evade the line of fire.

Solidly trap the weapon arm and weapon
with your arms and hands.

THE SPIRAL DISARM

An understanding of the weapon's line of fire must be maintained at all times when dealing with a firearm. Beyond the importance of clearing the line with your own body, you must also maintain awareness of where the weapon is ultimately pointing. Bullets can hit friends, family, and innocent bystanders. We will, therefore, classify our firearms according to the range of movement applied to the weapon.

Naturally, the more people you have in your surroundings, the more tightly you will have to control the line of fire, limiting many of your options. We will refer to the angle directly in front of you when you are standing square noon, to your immediate right three o'clock, your back six o'clock, and so on. In our first scenario, we will imagine a room of innocent people around you. You have your back virtually against a wall, so you are certain that roughly five to seven o'-clock are clear. Of course, no technique can prevent the possibility of ricochet, and the possibility still remains a stray bullet can harm innocents, but this is the most that can be done in such a circumstance. As always, we seek to blade, zone, fence, load, breathe, and use our eyes tactically. Immediately engage the aggressor verbally. If he had only wanted to kill you, he would have shot. Whether he is looking for respect, wants something from you, or is hesitating, there is a window of opportunity. Do not compete with the aggressor. Do everything that you can to show compliance and respect.

TRAINING TIP: When raising your hands against a gun or knife that is near your face, remember that the inside of your aggressor's weapon arm is more visible to him. The outside is slightly occluded by his arm. When raising your arms, be sure to raise the arm on the inside of your attacker's field of vision more slowly. Keep more distance and show full submission to avoid triggering his suspicion. Raise the outside arm closer to his gun arm, keeping it low and to the angle where the aggressor's field of vision is partially blocked by his own arm. In addition, using slow gestures with the inside arm can be helpful in leading the aggressor's attention away from your second hand. I think of slowly framing his attention between my inside hand and eye contact. This is particularly important if you are trying to calm someone who is in a heightened emotional state or is chemically altered.

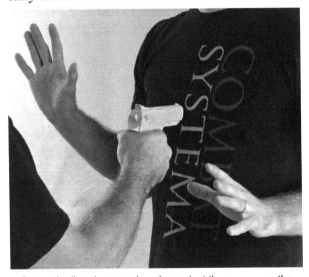

Strategically raise your hands against the weapon—the outside hand is more hidden from the attacker and can therefore be closer to the weapon arm for an efficient counter.

The first disarm is what we refer to as a "spiral strip." Evading always from the body a fraction of a second first, think of deflecting the weapon with the front side of your body when it is in contact with you or with the frame of your forearm when it is slightly farther away. Throw your lead elbow over the weapon arm, clamping both hands around the wrist and step deeply into the aggressor. As you lunge forward with your lead foot toward the noon position, pull his gun arm straight away from his body toward the six o'clock position, ramming into his ribs. Simultaneously twist the weapon away from your body, keeping the line of fire stable. It should be as if the barrel of the gun were a screwdriver putting a screw into the six o'clock position. Clamp your armpit deeply onto the subject's triceps and sit into him.

When applying an arm bar of this type, biomechanically we seek to raise the arm up to 45 degrees and then forward toward the opponent's head to 45 degrees. This ratcheting action greatly weakens the shoulder. In the case of firearm disarms, attention must be placed on controlling the line of fire. For an added challenge, try to sink powerfully into his triceps to, in effect, push his shoulder down lower than his elbow. Similarly, by squeezing the arm in toward your ribs while pulling on it with your hands, you can, in effect, steer the aggressor's body to achieve the 45-degree forward angle by moving his body in tandem with the arm rather than just moving his arm. From the brace position, you can counterattack with knees and kicks to the legs, or reverse elbows to the face with the close arm. To strip the weapon, grip the gun from the top rear corner with the close hand, forcefully continuing to twist it in the same direction as the arm as you pull it straight toward the barrel.

The subject holds the gun near you.

Twist to evade the line of fire while
pushing and grabbing the gun.

Maintaining your grip, twist the subject's arm,
sliding your elbow over his arm and solidly
trapping his triceps under your armpit.

Grab under the gun hand with your free hand. Keep your
ribs tightly against the subject's ribs, with his arm deep in
your armpit and apply pressure to the twisted arm.

With your second hand, grab the gun and twist it, keeping the barrel pointing in the same direction.

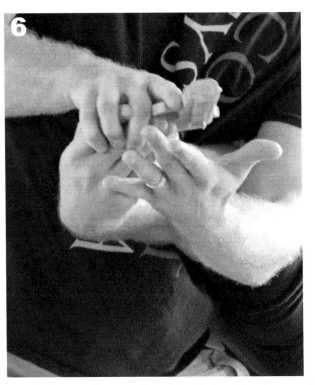

Doing so will cause the subject to lose his grip.

Aim the weapon with the free hand and step away to a safe distance—ideally, at least 9 feet (3 meters).

EXERCISE 84
WALKING THE DOG

Begin by acquiring an arm bar on your training partner. Practice intentionally steering his line of fire around the clock, from six to nine to noon to three and back, and then reverse the direction. This simple drill will help you appreciate the basic control potential of the lock. Remember the goal is to arrive with the barrel of the weapon facing each target position while it is 45 degrees above the subject and 45 degrees forward, toward his head, to place the arm in a position of optimal weakness.

For a second phase, practice bringing the subject to the ground from each position. To do this, slide forward with your nearer leg and sit down directly, replacing your lead foot with your buttocks. When you arrive, be sure that the arm is again 45 degrees up and forward. The steering drill can be repeated on the ground, crawling with your legs as you steer the arm and body around the clock.

From an arm bar position, you may drag the subject easily into a different position by taking a single step and twisting him around your trunk.

You can also slide your close leg through and sit to drive your weight against his elbow.

From the ground, you can explore the steering drill and perform a spiral disarm.

Pin his elbow to delay him while you get to your feet and move to a safe distance.

THE TRIANGULAR DISARM

In some cases, there is no safe angle to deflect to. There could be innocent parties all around you. You might also feel overwhelmed and unable to keep track of others. In this case, the objective is to turn the line of fire as quickly and efficiently as possible back toward the attacker, disarming him in the same motion.

To learn this disarm, evade and deflect, securing the wrist of the weapon-holding hand with your closest hand. Slide your free arm along your body to grab the weapon as close to the trigger (and as far away from the nozzle) as possible. Keeping the subject's wrist absolutely stable (your fulcrum) and applying pressure to the inside of the wrist to encourage flexion, sharply turn the tip of the gun back toward the subject's elbow. The attacker will try to move his hips or flare his elbow to compensate for the force and maintain alignment, so it is very important that you keep strong control of his wrist and keep your elbow anchored on your torso to stabilize him. This is often referred to as a triangular disarm because of the shape created; the subject's forearm is the baseline. Through the leverage provided by the gun, you seek to bend the subject's wrist to 90 degrees to create the right angle, and then by moving the nozzle directly toward his elbow, you create the hypotenuse.

Many styles teach wrist compressions in large circular actions. This is generally more in keeping with an overall ideology of flow, blending, or harmony rather than purely biomechanical and tactical considerations. If you are trying to bust the hinge on a door, you slam it straight back against itself. You do not lift and snake and try to twist the door off. Tactically, if you are trying to contain the line of fire, you either yield to the existing line and brace it during the disarm (as we did during the spiral disarm) or inhibit the trigger pull. By driving the weapon straight back into the attacker, the psychological motive to not shoot is obvious, but mechanically you are also robbing his grip of power.

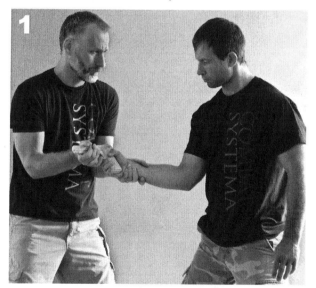

Evade the line of fire and firmly
secure the weapon with two hands.

Holding his wrist stable, twist the barrel of the
gun 90 degrees to the inside of his arm . . .

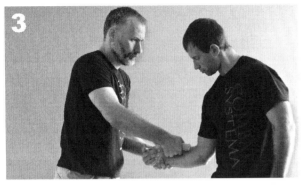

. . . and then directly to his elbow to weaken his grip.

Sharply jerk the pistol into his grip and then rip it free, driving it directly into his face.

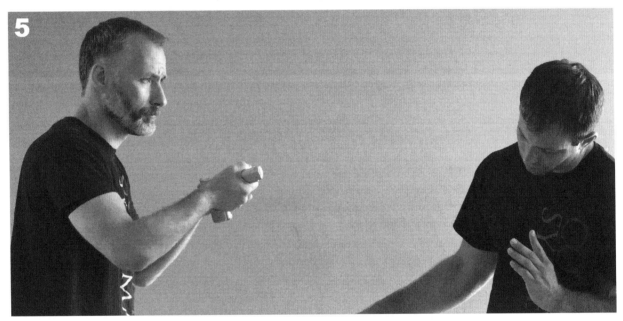

Pass the gun directly to your free hand . . .

. . . and adopt a close-quarter shooting position, where the pistol is beyond his comfortable reach.

EXERCISE 85
STEALING THE SQUEEZE

Extend your fist in front of you with the thumb up and squeeze as hard as you can for the duration of your exhale. Now relax and flex the wrist 1 inch toward the back of the hand. Freeze there and squeeze as hard as you can. Walk the knuckles back another inch and repeat, continuing until you are at the maximum flexion of your wrist. Return to center and repeat the progression toward the inside of the wrist. You will see that at both extremes, your grip weakens as you near your maximum flexion. This is something that can be improved, and through this drill and others we do consciously cultivate dynamic flexibility, but this simple exercise clearly illustrates how the triangular disarm begins to inhibit the trigger squeeze.

The triangular disarm can also include a small linear jerk at its end. Sometimes, after completing the initial twist, the grip will have adapted somewhat and the aggressor may still be hanging on without being functional on the trigger. Punch the nozzle briskly toward his face or body, hitting him, and pull the weapon straight back toward you to strip it completely.

The triangular disarm is usually performed on a lateral plane when the gun is level with the torso. Flexion to the outside of the attacker's wrist also runs the risk of breaking his trigger finger, so be careful during training.

Squeeze in correct alignment.

Squeeze fist while flexing the wrist outward.

Squeeze fist while flexing fist inward.

THE VERTICAL DISARM

When the weapon is higher, the strip usually occurs upward, with the hands coming from underneath the weapon and the nozzle being driven straight back to the medial line of the elbow joint. To best perform this, clear the weapon and secure it with the nozzle pointing over your shoulder to one side of your head. Brace the elbow of the gun-gripping hand tightly against your ribs and lean your head away to protect from muzzle blast. From a loaded rear foot, drive the gun-side shoulder forward. This will optimize your power and can allow you to strike with the elbow to the chest or face. The sights of the weapon can also be used to rake the attacker's face.

Performing the vertical disarm on a downward trajectory is very rare. Imagine someone had driven the gun into your pubis, your hands were above it, and you were forced to drive it straight to the ground. Rather than wrestle from this inferior position, train yourself to clear the weapon and then deflect it to a lateral position for a stronger disarm.

When performing a disarm, it is essential that you are always driving into the aggressor to unbalance him. Do not pull on the weapon because this will allow the attacker to easily center the weapon back onto you with a small squaring of the hips. Drive and strike, kneeing into the legs, head spearing into the face, and elbowing while maintaining control of the weapon to overwhelm him for a moment before attempting the disarm. If you encounter initial resistance on one plane of movement, switch the disarm to an alternate angle, moving horizontal to vertical or vice versa.

The subject holds the gun high against your neck.

Evade the line of fire, apply outside hand to the wrist as the fulcrum . . .

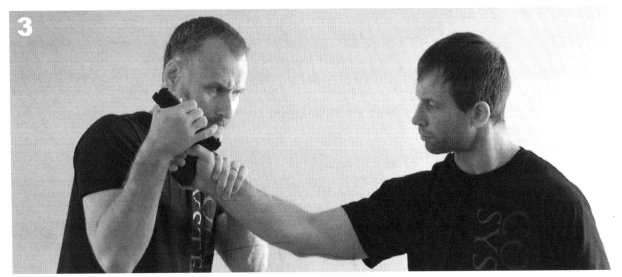

. . . and grab the gun as close as possible to the trigger with the inside hand, pointing the nozzle over your shoulder.

 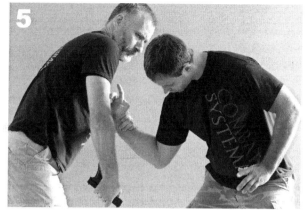

Holding his wrist firmly in place, roll your shoulder forward for optimal power—drive the barrel vertically upward and then downward toward the elbow joint to loosen his grip and then straight down to disarm him completely.

Spike the attacker in the throat with the muzzle to stun him.

Transfer the weapon to your free hand for readiness of use; clear and adopt a close-quarter shooting position.

FOREARM SCISSOR DISARM

The forearm scissor is widely used when the firearm is being held to your back or your side and you begin in a low frame. It is always a good idea when beginning to practice defense from new positions, whether they be rear attacks while seated or kneeling, to start by isolating the push and yield drill. By doing this from behind, you will notice that your spine serves as the axis of all movement. Contact with your right side should motivate you to rotate to your left, and vice versa. Rotate to evade the line of fire. During the rotation, the outside of your upper arm will serve to provide the initial deflection of the firearm. Rotate the deflecting arm around the attacker's forearm, turning your thumb downward so that the radial bone digs deeply into the muscles of his arm. A very common and costly mistake is to squeeze with the inside of your forearm. This tissue is soft and does not cause the aggressor pain, is easier to slip out of as a result, and leads to flexion in the wrist, which lessens the total force being applied. Trap the weapon arm against your chest, clamping it in place with your free hand. Do not push the arm downward toward the elbow, as this will cause the arm to slide down and the weapon to center with your face and head. Instead, inflate your chest and pull your forearm directly into it. Any downward motion should come only during the counterattack through a correct pivot and not by leaning forward. Do not interlock your fingers. Instead, clasp your hands together, palm-to-palm for optimal power.

From the forearm scissor trap, you may deliver head spears, knees, and stomps, and, most important, elbow strikes to the face and throat without weakening your grip. These can also be used to drive the opponent forcefully to the ground to achieve a butterfly pin and finish.

To strip the weapon from a standing position, slide the support arm up along your chest and the side of your face. Contact with your body is an important training detail that will train you to avoid the line of fire. Do not reach directly to where you think the gun is, as spatial awareness can skew increasingly under actual stress. Grab the gun and perform a triangular disarm.

TRAINING TIP: When defending against the gun or knife, particularly when it is thrust into your side or back, a common initial reflex is to flinch away and weaken contact, as if you were ticklish. This costs you valuable kinetic awareness. If this occurs, any attempt to regain solid contact must be justified by your behavior. This can include showing signs of submission, asking questions to distract the subject, nodding and making eye contact to show you are listening and understanding, and masking any movement toward the gun in subtle, natural gestures. Nervously puckering away from the weapon can trigger anxiety in the attacker and get you shot. Leaning subtly into the weapon gives the aggressor a stronger feeling of control, as if you were almost impaled by the weapon. It will also allow you to evade the line of fire more quickly, by essentially falling to one side of the line. When the subject lacks solid contact with the barrel, he often lurches forward within the line of fire first, reflexively, and gets shot.

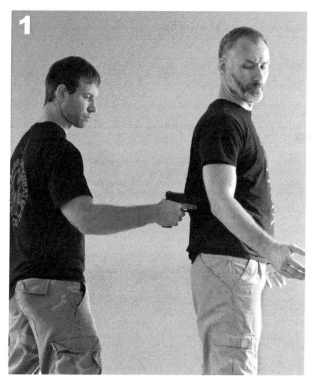

The attacker drives a gun into your back. Show submission while keeping contact with the gun's nozzle.

Maintaining contact with the nozzle, evade the line of fire by rotating toward him, using the closer arm as a deflection but keeping his arm close.

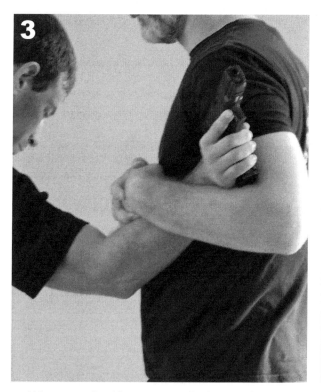

When wrapping his weapon arm with your forearm scissor, do not press with the softer inner forearm.

Instead, clasp your hands palm to palm and drive the sharp edge of your forearm into his wrist.

Always drive forward, using head spears, knees, stomps, and elbow strikes to unbalance him, making it easier to disarm him.

To disarm, sweep your hand along your body as if you were washing it to avoid crossing the line of fire.

Grab the pistol firmly and perform a triangular disarm.

Finish the altercation by switching the weapon to your other hand for readiness of use; use knees and other strikes to weaken the assailant; clear and move to a close-quarter shooting position.

EXERCISE 86
SHARPENING YOUR SCISSORS

To train yourself to have a confident and powerful forearm scissor, have your partner lie down on his back. Stand over him, with one foot on either side of his waist. Squat down as he extends one arm upward toward your face. Acquire the scissor powerfully and practice squatting up and down, lifting your partner off the ground. Be sure to keep your tailbone engaged and your ribs braced against your spine. If this proves to be too painful to the subject's forearm, you can insert a focus mitt between your arms to make it extra slippery and challenging.

Stand over your partner and wrap his forearm with yours, digging the radial bone into the muscles of his arm.

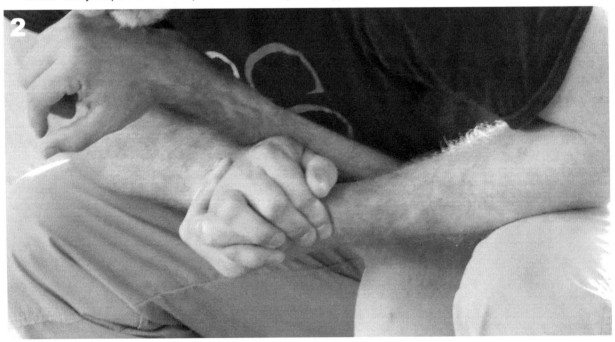

Clasp your hands palm to palm and pin his forearm on your chest.

Holding his arm firmly with your forearm scissor, squat up and down raising him without letting his arm slip. Keep your tailbone engaged and your ribs braced, lifting from your legs, not your back.

THE OVERWRAP

The final type of gun trap I will address is the overwrap. This is my least favorite type of trap for control. If you dwell in this position, a subject can too easily rip his pistol out of your grip and shoot. I use the overwrap most often for gun threats from the side or back, when my arms are in a high starting position. From there, yield exactly as you did for the forearm scissor, but this time the close arm will simply wrap over and secure the top of the weapon arm. Gripping the elbow or triceps with the palm is generally stronger. To assist fighting the aggressor's desire to pull the weapon back, drive forward with a counterattack with your free arm. When putting the aggressor down, you may wish to maintain the arm wrap and squat deeply or to carefully slide into a butterfly pin, feeding the gun hand to your free hand.

With your arm wrapped over your partner's gun arm, constantly drive forward and deliver strikes with your free hand and elbow.

If you lack pressure on his arm, he may be able to screw the pistol back toward you.

In that case, immediately blend into a Russian 2-on-1 to neutralize his weapon arm.

In case he pulls his wrist out of your grab . . .

. . . rotate toward him, sliding the arm holding the triceps down to the loose wrist and underhook the triceps with the inside arm.

Keeping forward pressure, drive the weapon into him to stabilize the weapon and destabilize him.

Then bring his weapon arm to the outside of your hip, into an inside Russian 2-on-1, always driving forward.

Switch holds again, overwrapping his arm with your outside arm, keeping the weapon behind you and returning to the initial overwrap position.

Once his arm is secured behind you, proceed with counterstrikes of your choosing and an overwrap takedown.

EXERCISE 87
GUN SENSITIVITY

From the overwrap sweep, practice controlling your subject with your knees and feed the gun hand from a wrap to a wrist grip and back to an overwrap on the far side. For an added challenge, you may wish to also practice moving to north-south kneeling or three-point control as you manipulate the arm and even move to the front of the aggressor to work arm bars. Perform one three-minute round of exploration without resistance, one round at medium resistance, one round at full resistance, and then a final round with little to no resistance to allow yourself time to practice what the pressure-testing taught you.

LONG GUNS

A common mistake in considering defense against long guns is to consider the length and the leverage it provides only from a defensive context. The reality is that long guns will generally be held with two hands whereas pistols may or may not be, and those hands on the long guns will be farther apart, providing greater control. The weapon butt will generally be braced against the body, and the overall control advantage of the weapon because of the length goes to the wielder not the defender.

EXERCISE 88
EDUCATING THE ATTACK

A common tactic taught is to evade the line of fire while grabbing the barrel of the weapon and pushing it off the line of attack. Working with a partner, slowly practice this action, working at medium speed and locking your grab in place. Then, have the attacker practice simply pulling his hip backward on his open side, stepping back slightly to adjust his balance, in order to bring the line of attack back on his subject. You will notice that with very little force, the gun wielder will generally be able to point the weapon back on his target. Take this further now. An attacker with a gun does not want to be close. If he is at this distance, he is likely to be extremely cautious and primed to shoot. The moment he sees movement, he is likely to fire and retreat, or move laterally.

Now practice the same grip, sandwiching the barrel with both hands. The grip will be stronger, but the second hand is more likely to pull in this position rather than push. If your ag-gressor lowers his base or falls onto his back into a prone shooting position, the weapon will be dragged automatically back toward you. If a struggle ensues in a standing position, the nozzle will most commonly be directed wildly upward, now effecting a larger zone of fire. Moreover, if you wish to move inward toward the attacker and "climb" the firearm, you are faced with three less than ideal options:

- You can keep your grip pivoting your body inward, which in effect offers your back to the attacker and only really sets up huge circular disarms that permit wild firing.
- You can keep the grip with your top hand and strike with your back hand with a criss-cross arm position, which robs you of power and limits how far you can enter.
- You can keep the grip with your bottom hand and move in more deeply, but now you are effectively only controlling upward resistance of the gun with a single thumb, which is likely to be insufficient.

Failing counter 1: avoid grabbing the barrel with one hand and pushing it away.

The attacker can too easily pull his hips back to center the weapon back onto you.

Failing counter 2: similarly, driving the barrel straight up offers fleeting control.

Trained attackers can simply fall to the ground to center the gun back on your mass.

Failing counter 3: a common error during disarms includes turning your back to your subject.

Failing counter 4: awkward cross-body movements rob you of your power.

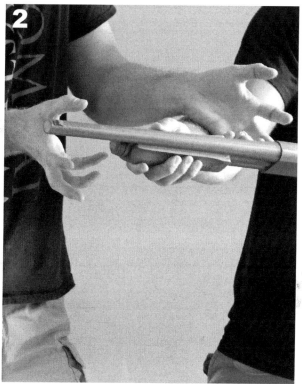

Failing counter 5: another mistake is trying to control the long gun with a palm-up grip, which essentially pits your thumbs against the leverage of the gun.

Next, practice achieving a "bicycle grip" with both hands side by side, palms downward as if you were grabbing a set of handlebars. Now the grip will likely feel stronger still. The weapon is less likely to be steered upward in this grip. Because both hands are palms down, you will be leaning and pushing downward rather than pulling upward. The far hand is better able to brace the gun against your hip, freeing your close hand to climb inward and better smother your partner's ability to retract the weapon.

Some options include:

• Deliver a circular elbow to the attacker's face as you step through his baseline, thus disrupting his structure. Envelop the weapon with your inside arm, tucking it deeply into your armpit and sinking downward on the weapon. From this position, the full power of your trunk can be applied to the weapon to twist the gun out on a horizontal plane. You will have the rifle immediately primed to fire.

• Drive across the attacker's face or throat with your forearm. Step on or behind his rear foot and drive him backward to his triangle point. Maintain control of the nozzle, supporting it further with your closer thigh or knee. From here, you may stomp or drop your knees onto the subject while maintaining full control of the gun.

• Climb inward and wrench the rear hand off the trigger using an underhook. From here, you can use your knee to pry the lead hand off the nozzle and drive the attacker away to acquire control of the weapon.

FIRST GOOD OPTION

Try a basic bicycle grip that allows you to exert your weight on your attacker's weapon.

Drive into your attacker with a devastating elbow and powerfully wrap the gun with your armpit.

Using your hips, twist back toward the attacker while stepping away and tear the weapon free.

Gain distance and acquire a shooting position.

SECOND GOOD OPTION

Evade the line of fire and drive into your opponent with a strike as you step behind him. Maintain control of the nozzle at all times.

Standing solidly, sink with your hips and drive him back and around your lead leg.

Keep the line of fire away as your opponent falls and, moving with his centrifugal force, rip the weapon away.

Acquire a shooting position.

THIRD GOOD OPTION

Evade to the inside of the attacker and hold the nozzle of the gun with your closer hand. Use a hammerfist to create an opening of the trigger arm to acquire the underhook.

Thread your hand under the armpit as you drive forward.

Pry his elbow high to force it away from the trigger, and twist back to wrench the weapon away.

Peel the attacker's fingers off the trigger and push him away.

Clear the attacker and assume a shooting position.

FOURTH GOOD OPTION

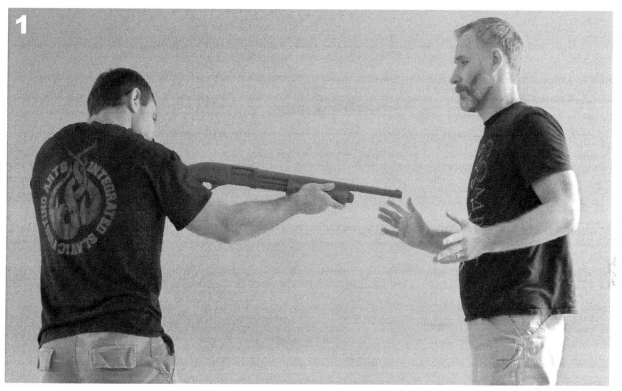

Your attacker levels his weapon at you.

Clear the line of fire and drive forward vigorously, sandwiching the weapon between you.

Brace his back as you drive his chin back over his shoulder and
step forward, driving his head to the ground with a violent smash and neck twist.

FIFTH GOOD OPTION

Wait for a moment of distraction to enter.

Deflect the weapon and drive
in in order to unbalance the attacker.

Clamp your hands viciously around his head and wrench it away from you to steer the line of fire away.

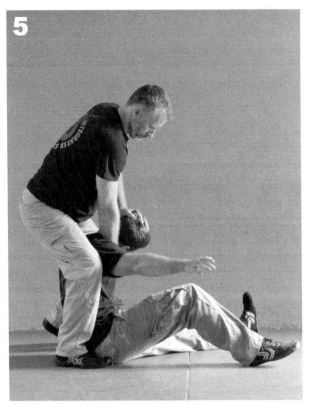

Sit him down violently and plunge
his head directly to his groin to injure his neck.

Step forward to sit explosively on the
back of his head for devastating power.

SECTION

8

USING IMPROVISED WEAPONS

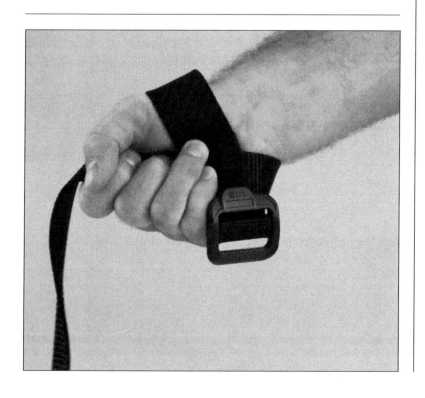

Our everyday environment is full of potential weapons. From the clothes we wear to the tools we use to the furniture in the rooms we spend time in, weapons are everywhere. When you are attacked, correct training should prepare you to maximize the full capacity of your surroundings. Improvised weapons provide a powerful psychological advantage. They empower the user and help thwart the onset of a sense of being victimized. They likewise can surprise the attacker and respond to his threat with a higher degree of risk than he anticipated. Every attacker and defender have a calculus of violence—an equation determining how much damage they wish to inflict and how much harm they are willing to incur to inflict it. When improvised weapons are brought into play, the formula can get briskly shaken, and formerly timid-looking defenders can become unpredictable, formidable, and difficult to gauge.

PENS

Let's start with the common pen. Available practically everywhere, pens can be carried easily, deployed quickly, and used without being seen. The first rule of using any improvised weapon is to learn how *not* to use it and how to function despite having the tool in your hand. People tend to obsess over improvised weapons and fixate on employing them rather than using them as a complement to their total arsenal.

EXERCISE 89
IGNORING THE WEAPON

Holding a pen in your preferred hand, practice lightly wrestling with a partner. Study how you are able to control the partner, striking him, steering him, and putting him down with a finish, all without using the pen or the hand it is in. This exercise is a fantastic limitation drill for awakening the potential of the remainder of your body. Practice for at least one round of three minutes.

A pen can make a very effective improvised weapon.

Orthodox pen grip.

Ice pick pen grip.

For your second round, begin implementing the pen as a distraction or bait. Practice manifesting the object and faking with it, but then engage exactly as you did in Exercise 89, without using the pen or the pen hand itself.

Use the pen to distract the subject's attention (top) and set up the sucker punch (bottom).

For your third round, begin integrating the use of the pen. Do not overrely on it; simply use it when it is natural and effective. A good way to make a training pen is to remove the ink tube from a plastic ballpoint pen (this prevents a mess in case the pen should crack in training) and cover the pen in a layer or two of duct tape. This will prevent sharp shards of plastic from going into the skin or onto your training surface, thereby providing you with a very cheap and easy improvised weapon.

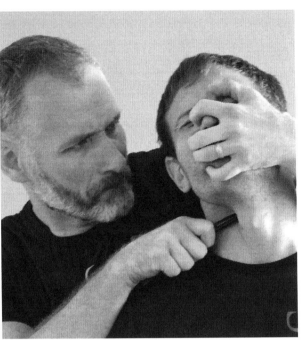

Using the pen.

When using a pen, you must respect the strength of the tool itself and use it according to its capacity. A disposable plastic pen should be largely covered by the hand, with only the smallest nub protruding to prevent it from breaking during use. Stronger steel pens or, better yet, specifically designed tactical pens, kubotans, or similar self-defense key chains or pocket flashlights can be allowed to jut out more significantly. The simplest use of the pen is to augment the power of a hammerfist. Short strikes or rakes to the face and throat are devastating, and strikes to the hands can sometimes be damaging as well. Shots to the body, however, will be largely muted by heavier clothing. During your training, practice accessing your pen in a casual, non-studied manner. Adopt stances and gestures that allow you to move the pen unseen in your hands. If you are walking into a questionable area and have a pen readily available, or are answering an unexpected knock at your hotel door, a pen is easy to find and grab and can tilt the odds in your favor.

Holding the pen against your body, fold your second arm over to conceal it.

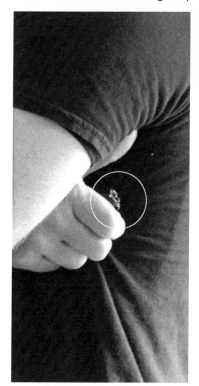

A close-up view with the thumb raised to reveal the position of the pen.

Since arms are folded and not braided, you can launch into quick strikes easily.

TACTICAL FLASHLIGHTS

Directly akin to pens are tactical flashlights. Generally, tactical flashlights are extremely compact, durable, and bright. They are often waterproof and shockproof, are faceted or equipped with stoppers to prevent them from rolling away, and have variable settings, including off, touch, and strobe features. In addition to all the tactics used with a pen, flashlights can also be used to blind and temporarily stun aggressors. Some basic training ideas:

- From a high shield position, practice flashing your light or hitting your strobe. As you hit the light, step forward and to one side. When blinded, attackers may launch their attack to your last-known position. Don't be there when it arrives. Step off the line as you lunge forward and then bounce inward into the aggressor, attacking by any means at your disposal.

- From a submissive, conversational stance, practice gesturing naturally with the flashlight in your hand as if it were a natural extension of your body. If your aggressor notices something in your hand and is distracted by it, use this to your advantage to improve your position. Practice suddenly flashing him as you launch into an ambush.

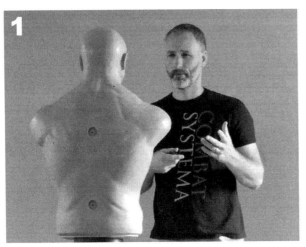
Holding the flashlight during a verbal de-escalation.

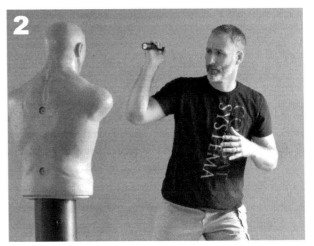
Zone away from the subject as you bring the flashlight into play.

Flash the subject's eyes.

Change levels as you drop forward and smash the subject with the light.

- When clearing a corner or walking into a new area, practice holding the light high overhead and trailing behind you. If there is an unseen attacker, he will shoot, stab, or punch toward a light. If you have the light in front of your face, you are likely to take the brunt of the damage. If the light is high overhead and you are squatting beneath it, there is a far better chance you will evade damage.

Peek around the corner, keeping your flashlight high but unlit.

Stay ahead of your light and move away from it as you light it.

Moving away from the light makes targeting you more difficult.

BACKPACK/ BAG/PURSE

Many people carry a bag or backpack every day. The first step is to practice wearing the bag in a manner that is solid, stable, and minimally disadvantageous to your posture. Backpacks should be slung fully onto the back and worn over both shoulders. Shoulder bags should be slung diagonally, with the bag portion tucked under your arm on your side or toward your front where you can see it and better protect it. This allows you dynamic and powerful movement without concern for loss of the bag. In training, having a replica bag heavily but safely stuffed with soft material is a good idea. Practice your stance, strikes, ground engagement, and other movements while wearing your bag.

EXERCISE 90
CASUAL TRANSITIONS

The next step is to practice putting your bag on and taking it off and transitioning through everything in between as gracefully and comfortably as you can. Make your action smooth and continuous. As you become more proficient, practice mindfully engaging your eyes to make eye contact with your training partner, adding smiles, squints, and other facial expressions to temporarily draw his attention away from your movement. Study how you are able to zone, blade, fence, and load your stance as you move the bag around your body and then repeat the study as you walk smoothly and comfortably. Every aspect of your daily life is an opportunity to put this training into action and increase awareness.

Practice wearing your backpack comfortably.

Insert your hand under one shoulder strap.

Slip the strap over one shoulder and allow it to swing around the body, catching it in front of you.

Hold the pack firmly in front of you to both shield yourself from being hit and use it to hit an opponent.

When using the backpack or bag as a weapon, keep your actions simple. Hold the bag solidly with both hands in front of your body, with your arms flexed and loaded. Study how you can ram, push, and deflect with the bag. Remember your basic principles and always focus on evasion first, using the bag as an aid to deflections and hits and not as a replacement for good movement. Like a matador's cape, the bag is only an assistance, not a magical weapon.

Avoid complex whipping or snaring actions. To throw the bag, tuck it solidly into your chest and throw it powerfully with both hands. As you throw it, use a basic zigzag step, moving forward off the line and then springboarding back into the attacker to avoid dwelling in one spot too long. Remember, your attacker will launch attacks to your last-known position when he panics and will have trouble tracking your movement as you advance.

Begin by holding the backpack.

Execute a solid two-handed throw
from your chest to your opponent's face.

Zone off the line.

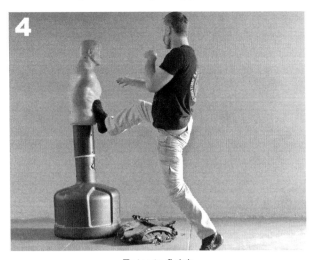

Enter to finish.

CHAIRS

While working as a doorman, chairs saved my life more times than I can count. Sometimes, it was a simple matter of being aware of the chairs in my environment as I stepped back and around them. Obviously, a chair could function as an object between an irate patron and me, giving me more space and time to defuse the situation. Other times, chairs served as a very physical shield and striking implement.

EXERCISE 91
IMPLEMENTING THE CHAIR

Stand up next to the closest chair available to you. Simply place your hand on the back of the chair and practice standing and shifting your weight in relationship to it. Imagine an aggressor approaching from any angle and study how you are able to simply step to put the chair between you and him.

Next, practice rocking the chair back onto one leg in the case of a stationary chair or rolling the chair with all wheels on the ground in the case of a wheeled chair. Study how you are able to squat, keeping your back straight, to grip the chair near the base of the backrest or the seat, leaning it against your thigh and waist and then, lifting with the legs, rock the chair backward, rolling it up your body, rather than trying to dead lift it straight up. Avoid placing a forearm across the seat of the chair. I have seen a knife split cleanly through a thick wooden seat with foam and vinyl cushioning. While the legs of the chair will do a lot to keep the attacker at bay, impact can occur with the seat. At most, keep one hand on the edge of the seat and the other on the backrest.

Keeping the chair solidly gripped and close to the body, practice stepping off the line and stabbing straight to the attacker's face and body. Avoid complex twisting motions. In the case of heavier chairs, simply flip the chair forward into the aggressor's footpath to delay him and step back on an angle to avoid having him fall onto you.

Stand behind the chair (front and side view).

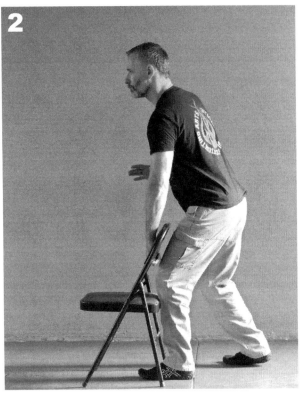

Squat and grip the back with your left hand.

Rock back, leaning the chair on your thigh.

Raise the chair with the help of your leg.

Use the chair as a shield (front and side view).

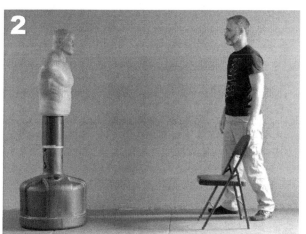 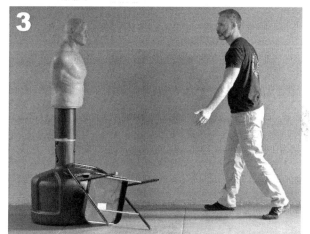

In the case of heavier chairs or less time, flip the chair into the subject's feet.

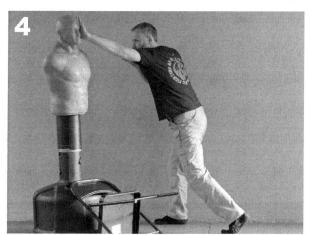

Left: Zone to the side and enter with strikes.

BELTS/ROPES

The belt and rope have a number of intriguing uses, many of them quite complex. I did my fair share of silat and kali, but I have found that the more complicated flexible weapon techniques erode under pressure. Remember the first principle: learn to operate despite the weapon. Let's avoid getting obsessed and keep things simple.

Although a belt can be an amazing advantage in a fight, taking it off at the wrong moment can get you killed. First, be sure you have the time and distance to remove it. Second, be sure your pants are able to stay up without it.

EXERCISE 92
BELT REMOVAL AND GRIP

Practice standing up and, without looking, casually unfasten and refasten your belt continuously. As you become more comfortable doing this without looking, begin to scan your perimeter, paying conscious attention to what is around you, rather than dedicating active thought to the belt.

To remove the belt completely, pull the buckle across your body slightly to gain a few inches of lead. Insert your free hand behind the buckle and then continue pulling. The support wrist will act almost like a pulley to help launch the belt out of the loops and can be used to offensively catapult the tip of the belt toward the attacker.

To secure an ideal grip on the belt, pinch the section just above the buckle with the pads of your fingertips to the meat of your thumb. Wrap the length of the belt through the web between your thumb and index finger and around your hand until it crisscrosses under the buckle again. Often, attackers can gain control of the other end of the belt during a fight. If the belt is simply wrapped around your hand in a conventional manner, it can ratchet tighter and get twisted, making it injurious to you and difficult for you to let go. By holding the belt in this manner, you will be able to simply untwist your wrist to release it at any point.

Many people are in a rush to swing the belt and whip with it. I strongly suggest you get some safety goggles and a tree or an old punching bag to test this out and calibrate your fantasies. The ornate figure-eights and fast, flashy nunchaku moves of the cinema erode in an often wild and less than fully controlled recoil on impact. For this reason, keep whipping actions simple and to a minimum. A good first step is to begin with a two-handed grip. When the second hand grabs the far end of the belt, there is no need to secure any special grip. Simply grab your belt, keeping your hands roughly shoulder-width apart.

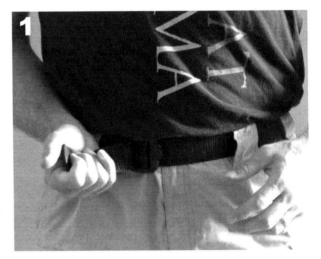

Open your belt.

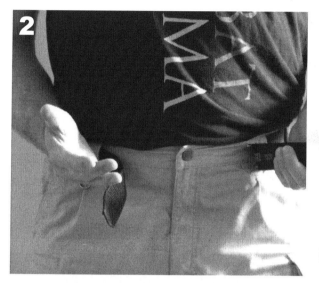

The belt is now ready to use.

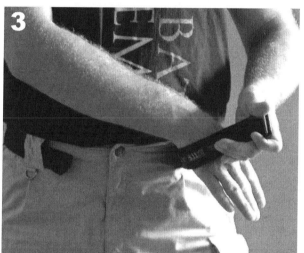

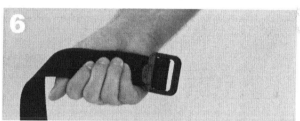

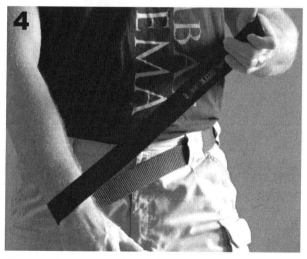

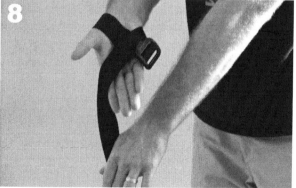

Hold the buckle, insert your free arm behind the buckle as a fulcrum, and use both arms to pull the belt.

To grip, hold over the meat of the thumb instead of in the web, wrap around the wrist, and fold over the buckle and up through the thumb web.

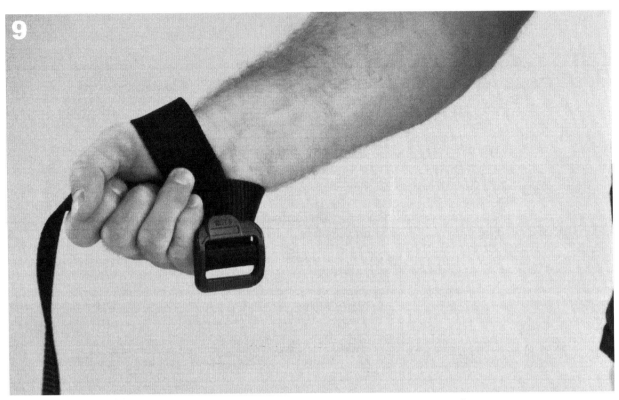

The belt is wrapped with less risk of snagging or getting caught.

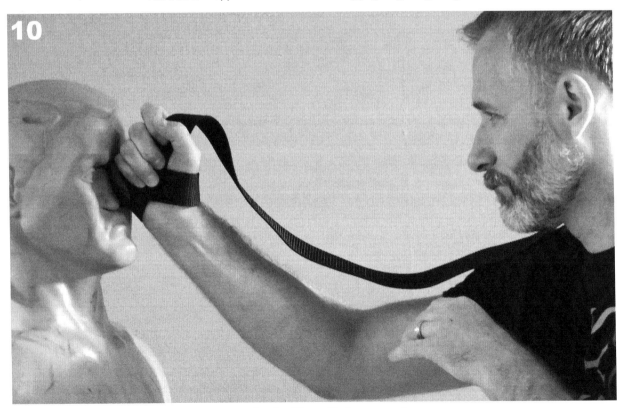

Example of striking with the pommel.

EXERCISE 93
THE TWO-HANDED SNAP

The first move is quite simple and can be used offensively and defensively. Have your partner extend a fist at stomach level, as if he were holding a knife frozen in space. Practice hitting the forearm just above the wrist with the two-handed grip. Keep a little slack in the belt and sharply pull either end of the belt outward as you pass his arm for the deepest impact. Snapping the belt too soon will rob you of power. As the movement becomes comfortable, have your partner begin slowly swinging so you can study how to time the interception.

Next, have your partner hold his forearm vertically to one side of his face to emulate a throat. Practice delivering the same hit by stepping forward and snap-hitting at the same time.

Practice snap-hitting the neck on your partner's forearm.

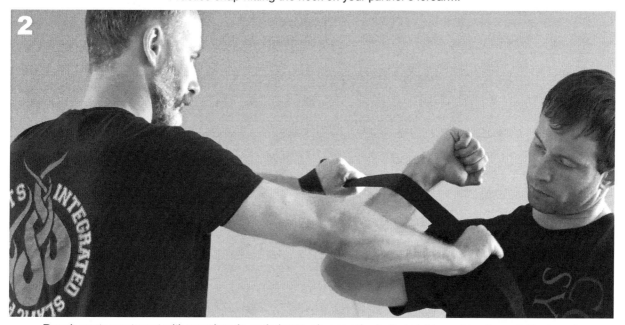

Reach past your target with your hands and vigorously snap the belt straight, pushing through the target.

This simple two-handed position can be easily adapted to complement many of the holds and locks that we have seen. One of the most natural is the underhook and pike. From the same downward hit-block we saw above, simply insert your outside arm as if you were going for a standard underhook. If your belt is long enough, you may still be able to pike the head; if you are unable to, simply drive the shoulder forward to the subject's triangle point to double him over. From there, you can effectively deliver knee strikes to his face or continue with a spiral takedown into a butterfly pin. Note than when the attacker lands on the ground, the belt will no longer be ensnaring his arm (it will be behind his hand) and you will need to hug the arm to

keep it in place. From that point, it is possible to wrap the wrist to snare it more tightly for a prolonged hold.

From the previous underhook, you can sometimes also thread the front length of the belt over the back of the subject's neck. This gives you powerful standing control and allows you the option of performing a spiral takedown again, ending with a hanging choke hold.

With the belt over the back of the subject's neck, you may also wish to simply maintain a nape control in order to better counterstrike. The nape control can also be converted into a choke during a throw or sweep, with knee pressure being added to the chest to amplify the effects.

While holding the rope with two hands, hammer your attacker's lead hand down.

Snake your left arm into an underhook and pull the rope tautly behind his neck, pushing his head downward.

Drive his head to 6:00 o'clock and pull his elbow up to noon.

Plunge him to the ground with a spiral takedown.

Pull the rope tight with your free hand to snare it.

Grab the loose end with your dominant hand for a tight trap and drop a knee into his head.

For an alternate takedown, pull the rope over the back of his head and around the front of his throat.

Pass the rope to your first hand and hold your attacker in an arm lock and choke, with one hand free to hit.

You can also pull his head down to the ground with the second end of the rope, pulling his head to the ground and around a second time for a crushing choke.

EXERCISE 94
BASIC WHIPPING STRIKES

If you do decide to resort to a one-handed position, keep strikes simple. Begin with the belt chambered over your shoulder and practice slowly whipping the belt on a downward diagonal angle, allowing the belt to swing freely under the free armpit so that the body can absorb the swing of the weapon. From that position, backhand strikes can either return along the same path on which they were delivered, chambering again above the shoulder as they arrive, or rise up on the opposite side and return on a downward angle so that they whip cleanly past the body. With a little practice, this can be blended into a fluid figure-eight motion.

Generally, it is easier to grip the buckle end of the belt. The buckle provides an excellent close-range striking and raking tool, and the empty end of the belt is far easier to control and less likely to injure you during the swing. Remember, at the moment of impact, the belt is likely to snake back toward you, so be sure to swing through completely with your hips and body to minimize this risk. When whipping with the belt, I strongly suggest abandoning any notion you may have of intercepting the attacker's arm or, worse still, ensnaring it. Primary targets should remain the face and throat. Whipping actions should stun and blind, elicit fear responses, and facilitate harder follow-ups and finishes. They are best reserved for bridging the distance.

Example of a figure-eight strike.

Whip on a downward diagonal.

Raise the belt back up.

Return on opposite diagonal,
making an X shape in front of you.

JACKETS

Jackets can be used in much the same way as a belt when they are being carried: to whip and snare an attacker. Although the extra mass tends to make them heavier and slower, the weight and surface area is generally more effective for deflecting if you wish to attack the limbs. Two-handed grips on jackets will provide less snap than hits with a belt but are better for netting and snaring the face and head and can be used to blind and stifle the subject. In addition, zippers and buttons can help cause pain as they inadvertently gouge the face or eyes.

When the jacket is being worn, the tails can be used to strangle the attacker quite easily. Begin with the corner of your jacket tail in your hand as if you were holding a knife. Pass the corner in front of the subject as if you were holding that knife to his throat. Grab it on the other side with the free hand and pull back. The first hand can now release and be used to half-nelson the neck and compress the head downward on the choke. This will be a combined wind and blood choke and is quite dangerous, so exercise care.

When your subject is wearing the jacket, the most effective way to acquire a choke is to slip under the subject's armpits on either side from behind. Grip the lapels of the jacket briskly on both sides of the neck and pull them forward with a snap, jolting the subject in the back of the neck to both stun him and ensure that there is no slack remaining. Release one side and reach deeply across to the other, cross-feeding it as high as the hand will go. Think of contouring the subject's throat with your second hand, bending the wrist to adhere as fully as possible to the round of the neck and tighten your grip. This hand should seek to grab as high as possible. Release the first hand and cross-reach with it lower on the other side, at clavicle level or lower. Begin pulling back and around with the high hand, as if you were drawing a happy face on the subject's throat. This will clamp shut the artery on that side. Pull straight down on the low side as if you were milking a cow. This will seal off the other artery. The most common mistake is to simply pull straight in either direction to crisscross the fabric. This will generally cause the two levers to tangle and compete, and can leave your opponent breathing room and cause you to needlessly expend energy. By tracing a happy face with the high hand and milking the cow with the low one, you give each lapel its own path and avoid this issue. Once this pressure is applied, you can pull the subject backward and lean forward with your shoulder to add compression to the windpipe as well or to compress the thorax and more safely impede the lungs.

Whipping with the jacket.

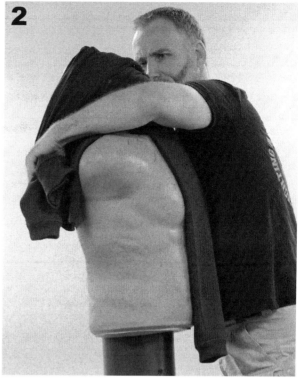

Two-handed ready position.

Two-handed jacket snare and hit.

Preparing to choke by flaring the collar.

Reach around the neck and under the collar, grabbing and pulling the collar tautly around the side of his neck.

Cross-reach with the second arm and grab the far lapel.

Pull the high lapel around his neck tightly and the second lapel straight down on a slight diagonal.

Grab the tail of your jacket.

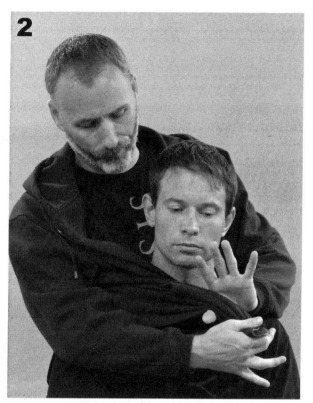

Cross-feed it to your second hand.

Pull the cloth firmly.

Reach under the close arm with your free hand.

5

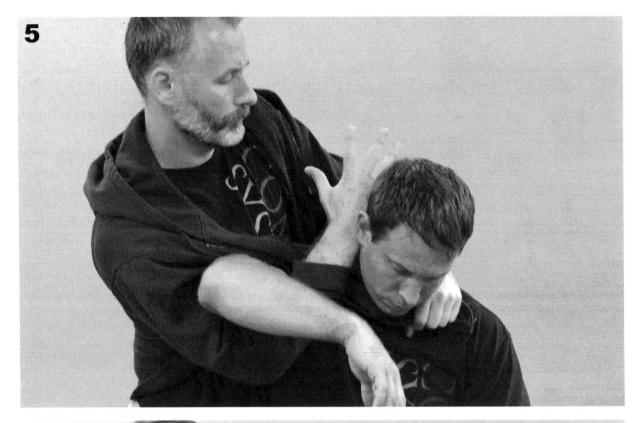

6

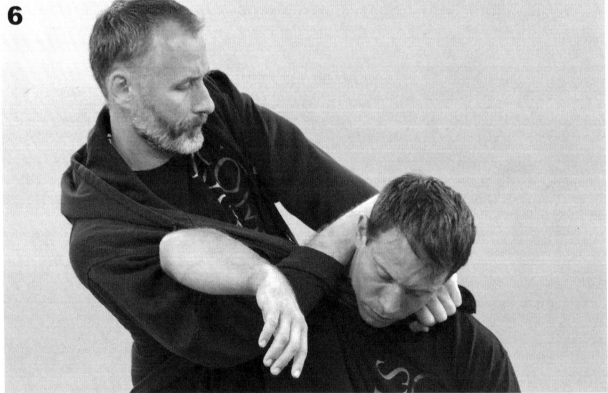

Snake your hand behind his nape and scissor the neck between your right arm and the lapel.

EXERCISE 95
THE CHOKE SIT-UP

A very simple and effective drill to master this choke is to lie on your back as if you were going to perform a basic sit-up with your knees bent and your feet on the floor. Take a jacket and wrap it around one knee, zipping it closed up the front of your shin and poking your knee out of the head hole. Practice performing a slow sit-up as you exhale. Freeze at the top and inhale as you acquire your grips for the choke. Exhale as you exert slowly and evenly. Release and roll back down as you inhale. Repeat this for three minutes. This will teach you how to calmly acquire the grips and exert while you are under increasing stress and fatigue.

Zip a jacket around your bent leg.

Practice sitting up and quickly acquire the necessary grip to choke your leg.

WALLS AND DOORWAYS

Two commonly overlooked aspects of improvised weapons are walls and doorways. Both are often available and can provide huge benefits if you are trained to use them correctly.

WALLS

It is widely expressed that keeping your back to the wall is a good way of preventing sneak attacks from behind. This is absolutely true, but, more than that, it is great for maintaining awareness of your surroundings. In my experience, people often move near walls in a conflict, feeling instinctively the safety they provide, but they fail to move close enough to them. As a result, in the heat of the moment, they reach back to cock their arm and smash their elbow into the wall, or try to take another step back and get tripped up when their foot is jammed. I have seen walls pockmarked with elbow holes, mirrors cracked, subjects bloodied, even individuals who bumped into a wall and looked behind to see "who" was behind them only to get sucker punched from the front.

EXERCISE 96
MAKING THE WALL YOUR FRIEND

When using a wall as a defense, move directly against it. Keep your feet a comfortable distance away and lean into the wall, flexing at the knees and sitting lightly against the wall. This will give you a certain and confident awareness of the wall and fully block your rear flank. Practice rolling the meat of your shoulders from side to side, leaning to your left and raising your right side off the wall, and then rolling back until the right side is stuck and the left extended. Focus on making the back soft and round, rolling the full surface comfortably without staying rigid and grinding your spine. You will notice this naturally rolling action is akin to a boxer slipping a punch and is a great way to create evasive movement.

The same action is also a great way to help jump-start your breathing. As we saw earlier, we can forget to move under conditions of stress.

Rolling the back on the wall in this manner is like an instant massage that helps knead the breath out of the lungs like squeezing a tube of toothpaste.

Rolling on the wall can generate tremendous power. Have your partner hold a set of focus mitts in front of you as you roll off the wall. The natural rolling action will generate amazing momentum for hitting. You can progressively have them step back and see how you are able to launch yourself farther, stepping with the same side as you strike. This will train the habit of cocking the arm and inadvertently hitting the wall completely out of you.

Another important aspect of wall movement is to crab walk. Keeping your back stuck and your legs flexed so that you are in effect lightly sitting into the wall, practice taking small steps to the left and right, sliding with your body. Avoid bringing the feet too close together and *never* cross them. This movement should be like a basketball player's defensive shuffle from one side to the other. Training this will get rid of the habit of stepping back into the wall.

Squat against the wall.

Roll to the meat of one shoulder.

Use the momentum to launch yourself off the wall.

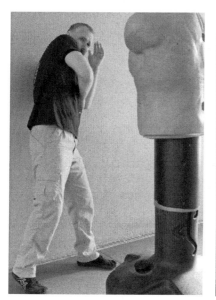  

Roll yourself from one side to the other and launch yourself forward with a strike.

EXERCISE 97
ADAPTING TO THE WALL

Any time you begin with a new weapon or stimuli, it is advisable to go back to the basic push versus yield drill prescribed at the outset of this book. Have your partner simply lean into you, pushing deeply until he is squishing you against the wall. Exhale and allow the pressure to relax your body and then slowly and softly roll the free side of the body forward. The obvious truth of the wall is that you cannot retreat on the affected side so you need to advance on the free side. Understanding this cognitively is simple—internalizing this at a reflexive level is quite different. Be sure to work very deeply and slowly here so that you can identify where you are twitchy and flinch, and to ensure that you are not continuously firing your nervous system in a way that either fights the push or the wall. Again, it is impossible to move too slowly—only too quickly.

When Muhammad Ali created the "rope-a-dope" against George Foreman in Zaire, the ring ropes were poorly installed and too slack, allowing Ali to lean back, in the words of journalist George Plimpton, "like a man leaning out his window trying to see something on his roof." This movement is impossible against a solid wall. The elasticity and give of the rope are also not present. The rolling and absorption must come from the lateral rocking of the body and to some extent a subtle springiness in the legs to transfer incoming force to the wall.

DOORWAYS

Directly connected to walls is the use of doors. Like columns, doors can provide a perfect funnel that reduces an attacker's options. When working inside a doorframe, the objective is to step back slightly, roughly a foot inside the frame. This will limit the effectiveness of large slashing motions and require the attacker to resort to more linear actions. Emphasis should be placed on sidestepping rather than retreating directly to maximize the advantage of the door for as long as possible. In addition, the doorframe itself can be used to smash the subject's limbs and body into it or as a painful fulcrum for locks. Naturally, the door itself can be used as well to hit and scissor the aggressor.

EXERCISE 98
MASTERING DOORWAYS

Working softly with a partner, practice having him encroach on you while you are near a door. If you are standing in front of the door, avoid stepping back blindly, as you can easily misjudge distance and orientation under stress. Take a small glance back with your peripheral vision without losing sight of your aggressor and reach back softly with your hands, like you might when guarding someone behind you in basketball. Practice stepping through the door to a sufficient distance. As your aggressor advances, study the best moment to intercept with finger whips, thrust kicks, and similar distance weapons, and slowly engage, studying how you can use the doorframe to your advantage. If clinching occurs, try to keep your body outside the doorframe, with the crown of your head driving into the subject's face and your mass pushing him into the frame like an MMA fighter might use the cage.

When you are encroached upon near a doorway, use your hands to feel your position relative to the door.

If time permits, retreat one step inside the door frame. This will funnel your attacker into delivering straighter attacks in order to reach you.

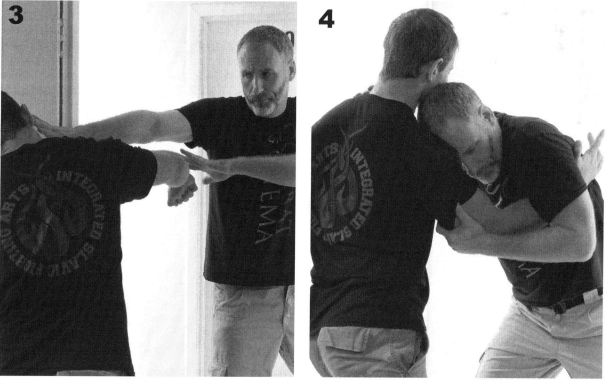

You can quickly counterstrike or clinch before the attacker can breach the threshold.

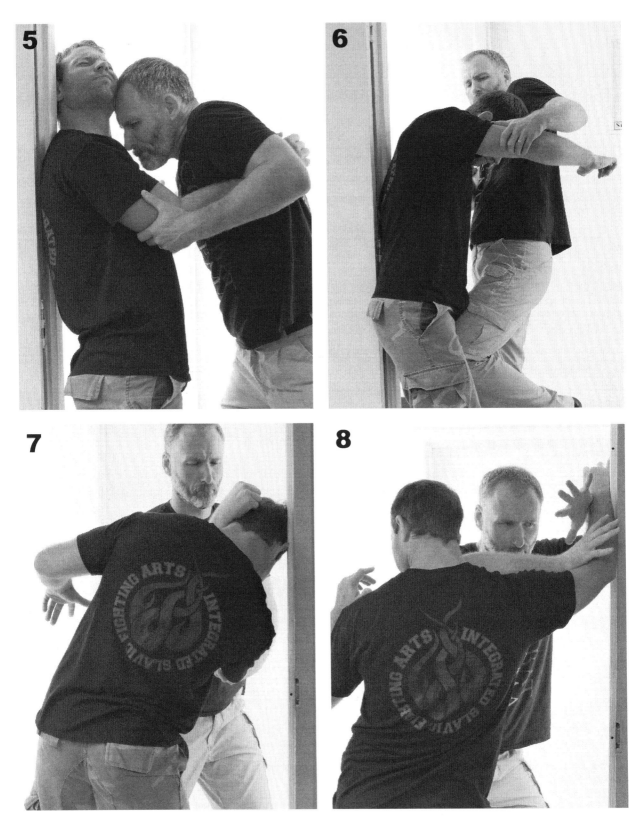

You can use the door frame as an anvil, driving your attacker into it with head spears or knee strikes, or you can smash his head or limbs into the frame or throw his limbs into the frame.

SECTION

9

MULTIPLE ATTACKERS

Dealing with multiple attackers requires specific training. Too often, practitioners wrongly assume that tactics that would otherwise succeed in sportive or one-on-one encounters will simply apply, when in reality, those tactics may work against them. In application, surviving two or more assailants requires continuous movement. Defenders cannot afford to dwell in the middle of a mob. If they get tied up in a clinch, all focus must be placed on striking, driving forward, and circling out of the group. This section will lay the groundwork for surviving multiple attackers and likely change the way you address seemingly single threats as well.

SLAVIC HISTORY OF MULTIPLE ATTACKERS

A consideration of multiple attackers and group fights is integral to Russian martial traditions. Slavic males often competed in mass fist fights during holiday festivals. Nestor the chronicler made the first known record of ritual fistfights in 1048. The most typical form was "wall fighting," wherein two lines of fistfighters would compete to strike through each other's lines. Other variations could include an outward-facing ring of fighters against a mob or even a free-for-all. These fights favored powerful striking. Striking was kept above the waist, with priority given to the head, solar plexus, and under the ribs. Striking downed opponents was illegal, and rules sometimes forbade striking a severely wounded or bloody opponent. Standing clinch work was permitted. Competitors were segregated by age, with boys, unmarried men, and married men competing separately.

The most powerful god in the Slavic pantheon was Perun—the copper-bearded, ax-throwing god of thunder and lightning. He was also the patron saint of the Russian martial arts, and mass fistfights were largely held in his honor. With the rise of Christendom in Russia, efforts were made to stifle all pagan rights. In 1274, it was publically decreed that participants would be excommunicated from the church and refused a Christian burial if they were involved in traditional fistfights. By 1641, punishments rose to include public beatings with rods, whipping, and even exile. Still, some lineages of the traditional arts have survived until this day.

EXERCISE 99
PREPARATION

As with all traditional Russian martial work, preparation begins with softening the body with contact. As the subject, you stand in the middle, with two to six partners standing around you in a ring. The partners begin pushing deeply and continuously at all heights of your body. As with the more basic versions of this exercise, the goal is to allow the pushes to lead you. Now, because of the sheer volume of stimuli, it will be impossible to predict where the force is coming from. You must let the forces simply move you without ego or judgment.

Work can evolve to having the partners push you vigorously enough to require you to take a step. Here, the body will adopt a more buoyant nature, often rising somewhat as you lift to step and dropping and flexing the knees as you land. This springiness will help dissipate the force and allow the largest portion of the push to pass through the body.

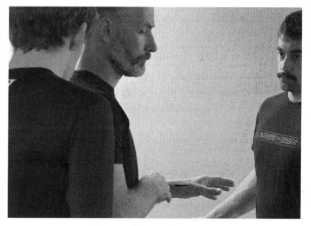

Encroachment by group.

UNDERSTANDING TRADITIONS

Traditional Cossack work is typically characterized by the following:

- Vigorous pivoting from the body helps maintain continuous reactive breathing, deflect incoming force from all sides, and generate power for counterstriking.
- A buoyant center of gravity that rises and falls to generate and absorb force while encouraging continuous movement rather than standing one's ground.
- Explosive whipping motions with the arms and, to some degree, the legs that employ elliptical and figure-eight paths in a continuous barrage.

Work was always designed to be easily adapted to single or multiple attackers.

EXERCISE 100
ESSENTIAL MOVEMENT

Begin by standing with your feet shoulder-width apart, knees comfortably bent, arms hanging in a low frame. Slowly, pivot one leg over. Emphasis should be to lead the motion with the hip, ensuring that you arrive with the ball of the pivoting foot solidly on the ground, the arch of the framing foot well planted and not rolling on the outward blade, and the center of gravity lower at the end of the pivot than at the beginning. Then return to center and pivot to the other side. Continue this slowly and mindfully, with the hips a little lower than normal, to burn the memory of correct movement into the legs. Breathing will be extremely cognitive here. Begin exhaling a second before you initiate your pivot and stretch it for the entire duration of the pivot. Begin the inhale a second before you return to center, stretching the breath and the movement so that you fill your lungs comfortably, without strain, as you arrive in the center.

Start in a comfortable position.

Begin your pivot by leading with the hip.

Whip the strike powerfully across the body, exhaling vigorously.

For the second phase, perform the movement more briskly. Focus only on a sharp, open-mouth exhale, as if you were blowing out a candle. Let the hip lead, pivoting quickly from one side to the other, from one pivot to the other, without dwelling in the middle. You should move as quickly as you exhale.

For the third phase, allow the arms to swing out as you pivot. You will notice that if you try to swing with the arms straight, they will become slower than your hips and you will be pivoting in the opposite direction before the arms have arrived in the first direction. This will break the unity of the body and add strain on the joints. By comparison, if you focus on whipping the elbows outward, leading with the humerus rather than the forearms, the arms will stay closer to the body and more synchronized and unified with your trunk. This will require less energy and provide faster deflections and counterhits in application.

EXERCISE 101
BODY INTELLIGENCE

Stand in the middle of a ring of training partners. For the first round, have the attackers only push and kick you in the legs. Begin slowly, with soft pushes, to allow you to loosen up. The importance of keeping the legs in alignment cannot be overstated here. Plunging up and down with the hips slightly will help load the legs and encourages correct alignment. When pivoting, the ball of the pivoting foot and support frame leg must be confident and solid. When moving, every step should be determined and heavy, as if you were trying to crush everyone's feet around you. The goal of this phase is to move continuously and efficiently rather than freeze up in the center where you will be an easy target. Naturally, this is an isolation phase, so we are dwelling somewhere we would not want to be for more than a second in application.

Yielding against group pushes.

For the second phase, you should actively try to counterstrike with the legs as they move. Take care not to prioritize hitting or you will again freeze up. Once more, the goal is to move constantly to be the hardest possible target you can be.

Leg push and kick versus a yield.

Leg yielding.

For the third phase, the outer ring should strike and push with the hands to the torso only. You should begin yielding only, playing with moving your arms between lower, middle, and upper frames as if you were washing your body. Perform the same rapid pivot and permit the arms to whip outward from the elbows. You will notice that the body will feel strong. You will rarely get hit squarely and, when you do, the force will be more easily dissipated. You will recover from winding more easily, and your whipping arms will begin to harm the strikers' arms, discouraging their desire to continue reaching inward. This phase is very much a game designed to break through a fear of contact. In a group training context, students will generally laugh and smile as they hit each other, which seems quite paradoxical at first. It is the first glimpse we get into the vigor, vitality, and strength of will that the early Slavs recognized these exercises created.

Torso punching.

Torso yielding.

For the fourth phase, you are permitted counterstrikes, whipping the elbows and hands out from the center as they yield. Protective helmets and mouthpieces are highly suggested, and care should always be taken here as these drills can escalate quickly.

Head tapping versus yielding.

Head tapping.

For the fifth phase, the attackers should prioritize open-handed slaps to the head only, and you should maintain high frames and wash your head vigorously as you continue to plunge up and down and to step and roll inside the ring.

For the sixth and final phase, you are permitted highline counterattacks, elbowing, punching, slapping, and more from the flow of your defensive movements.

EXERCISE 102
ISOLATING COUNTERATTACKS

As you will notice, all the odd phases of the previous drill were purely defensive while all of the even phases integrated counterattacks. It is beneficial to also drill the even phases in isolation so that you can practice unleashing your counterhits with more power. Situating yourself between two punching bags is all you need to practice moving continuously and striking. I strongly suggest isolating each phase, striking at first only with the legs and then isolating body counterattacks and finally the head before integrating them all in a fourth phase.

It is essential that we remember that each isolating phase is a gross exaggeration of small segments of a real fight. We are volunteering to dwell in hell at this point so that we can more rapidly and deeply condition our understanding and grow our familiarity with a fearful situation.

We must not confuse the drill with the application. A large aspect of the Russian martial approach to preparing for combat is to cultivate fighting skills and spirit along with a sense of community. These drills will quickly give students a rush of power and vigor and usually cause them to break out in nervous laughter and end with strong camaraderie if they are correctly performed. Traditionally they are practiced with music and a sense of competitive enjoyment.

Although traditional work is limited in application and only an isolation of small aspects of the total pie, it still contains a wealth of more complex strategies. Teams would have set leaders who would dictate strategies and formations. So-called fighters of hope were designated to break the enemy's rank and create openings by pushing, knocking down, or clinching multiple opponents to allow others to infiltrate the enemy line. Specialized strategies to counter them were used, which included baiting these attackers inside the line and then closing up behind them to cut them off from their teammates. Inside, experts in single combat would lie in wait to finish them off. For the modern practitioner, the most important aspect of this traditional work lies in those first few seconds of physical engagement. Priority must be placed on quickly and aggressively "cracking" the enemy line. We will expand on this idea shortly.

Flowing strikes from one target to another.

Rebounding with reverse elbow.

Flowing into a slap.

Driving into a Slavic hook.

CRACKING

In every encounter, emphasis must first be placed on preemptively improving your odds whenever possible. If the time permits to blade, zone, fence, load, engage your breathing, and maximize your sight, you must do this. If an opportunity presents itself to begin engaging the aggressors verbally, either to acquiesce or negotiate, then I strongly suggest that you do. Sometimes, however, it becomes apparent that the aggressors will not be satisfied. In other contexts there will be no time and you will simply be jumped. When this occurs, the first priority must be to get outside of the group.

EXERCISE 103
CRACKING THE MOB

Begin in the middle of a group of training partners, with your stance loaded, your fences up in a passive open-handed stance, and your energies dedicated to zoning and blading the collective and keeping the full group in your awareness. Have any member of the group initiate by interrupting you with a push. Immediately, bring your shields up, moving them continuously as if you were washing your hair, as the group unleashes a constant salvo of pushes and pulls. Use leg flexion, lower your center, and step with the pushes to absorb as much of the force as you can.

For the second phase, begin actively pushing into and rolling off the partners. Have them work to keep you inside with their pushes while you consciously try to build off the momentum they are giving you, by launching yourself through them. You will feel that holes will naturally form as one side pushes too hard, or as others are simply caught off guard and you will stumble out of the group. In the beginning, it is not uncommon to fall as you crack the group. If this happens, immediately revert to your ground defensive position and work to get back up onto your feet before you can be surrounded again.

For the third phase, have your partners hold kick shields in a ring around you. Have them take a step forward and shove you with the shields. As you shield and yield, practice rolling heavily into them, launching yourself and spiking them naturally from your defensive shields with the points of your elbows. This is an extremely dangerous phase and your elbows will hit powerfully, so be certain that everyone is holding their shields solidly.

For the fourth phase, have your partners hold focus mitts and stand at maximum distance, pushing and slapping with the mitts. As you yield and shield on the inside, practice whipping your fists, palms, and elbows into the targets. Remember that this is purely an isolation drill designed to emphasize how your shields and deflections can be weaponized. In an actual application, you will be seeking to exit the mob as quickly as possible. Whereas during the third phase, your goal was to dwell inside, in order to get as much counterstriking practice as possible, during the fourth phase, you should place emphasis on exiting the mob as quickly as possible as you hit.

Spike the first attacker with the elbow.

Rebound into the second attacker.

Absorb the attackers' pushes.

Shield and flow with the force.

Right: Charge the second attacker
to crack the mob and create an exit.

BODY SHIELDING

Once the mass attack is on, your priority must be to shield, yield, and crack the mob, getting behind the closest individual. Much has been said about the importance of taking out the leader in a group encounter to discourage the pack. While this may be effective in some preemptive circumstances where you are landing the first blow, once the fight is on, or when you are ambushed, there is absolutely no time. Attack the closest person immediately. Crack the mob as soon as you can. Get behind the nearest person and hold on using him as a shield by holding him by the hair or ears, raking the face and fish-hooking the lips, or pinching the fat and skin deeply to hold on. Grab his clothing if that is all that is available.

Traditionally, Slavic strategies included isolating and overpowering any warrior who showed greater skill or capacity. These fighters were often encircled or otherwise pulled from the front of the ranks by as many fighters as possible. In traditions where clinching or takedowns were prohibited, some contestants would crouch and drive forward around the fighter's legs to impede his mobility, much like a rugby scrum, while others would strike his exposed upper body from all sides. In much the same way, modern defenders should seek to fight one attacker at a time. Since we will rarely have the advantage of teammates, efforts should be made to move continuously particularly between obstacles whenever possible to force attackers to funnel toward you and fall into a single file where they can be addressed individually. In this context, body shields are fleeting opportunities. You generally can only maintain control for a few seconds once you have shocked them and their colleagues. Discard them hard, shoving them into the group and move immediately, fleeing to a better position as soon as possible or acquiring an improvised weapon.

EXERCISE 104
NATURAL HANDLES

Working with a partner, practice moving yourself behind him, "taking his back" as if you had singled him out while cracking the mob. Rather than trying to move the attacker around your center or steering his body at first, think of climbing up and around him, like a squirrel climbing a tree. The arms are natural starting points because they are how the attacker is going to try to keep you in the center of the mob. Climb up them like ropes, pulling them down the attacker's triangle point as you head-spear into his face. When you are ready to take his back, drive the arm in toward his hips and run around to take his side or rear corner before he can reset his position.

When driving in, most people have a tendency to lean forward, leading with the shoulders. By leaning in with your shoulders, you keep your hips 3 feet away from your attacker, who is effectively the "center" of the collective circle. As you try to move around him, you have a far larger circumference in which to run around. A 3-foot diameter is already giving you roughly a 9.5-foot circumference, which gives your opponent more time to react. If by comparison you drive your hips completely into your opponent's side, you are literally inches away from his back. Moreover, because you are stuck to him, you are better able to feel his movement and adapt more quickly than if you were depending on your eyes or the feeling communicated through his arms. Plus, by being on top of him in this way, you are immediately able to counter and stifle his actions.

Generally, you begin by dealing with the wrist or elbow in some variation of either a baseball bat grip or Russian 2-on-1 arm tie. From there, some natural handles include:

• Grabbing the aggressor's leg—usually grab the base of the thigh, just above the flexion of the knee. Avoid placing your fingers directly in the fold, as the fingers could be jammed and crushed if the leg folds.

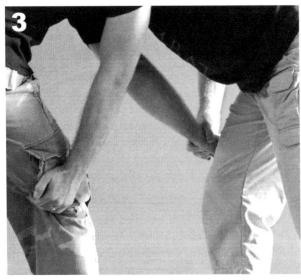

Common control tactics include ducking under the subject's armpit to take his back, pulling his wrist with a baseball bat grip to his triangle point, grabbing the tendons above the knee to pull yourself past the leg, stepping on his foot to delay his retraction, and grabbing the hip or lateral muscle to gain his back.

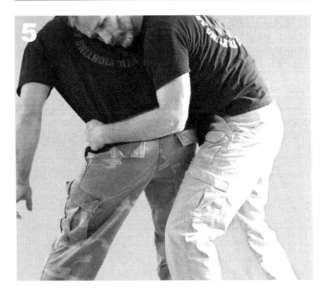

- Stepping on or near the foot is a good way of delaying his movement and moving in.
- Grabbing his belt or far hip is another solid way to limit his hips.
- Hooking the far lateral muscle or pinching the meat in that area is a good way of controlling the axial rotation of the shoulders.
- Grabbing the far-side trapezius muscle and reaching over for the throat, chin, or face are also excellent ways to climb in while affecting your attacker's mobility.

EXERCISE 105
THE HARD DISCARD

On the following page, once you have acquired the subject's back, you may be able to control him for a second or two, effectively using him as a shield against the other attackers, but more often than not, you will be required to abandon him to continue moving dynamically. While holding your shield, it is effective to keep your subject unbalanced with pain. Knee shots to the tailbone are a great way to shock his nervous system and hamper his mobility. Tight twisting grips that involve the hair or ears are also good, as are rapid rakes and gouges of the face. If you can get your subject to react in pain, you can begin to discourage the other attackers from continuing or at least make them begin to second-guess themselves.

When you are ready to discard the subject, a strong knee to the tailbone or a horizontal elbow to the back of the neck near the brain stem (or the floating rib if you are unable to reach the head) is a powerful way to incapacitate him and send him stumbling forward into the others. If the attacker is much larger, a straight upward shin kick to the groin from behind can crumble him and leave him blocking the way in pain. Keep hits simple, direct, and devastating when discarding the shield. Never simply release them.

In the end, multiple attackers are a challenging and dangerous dynamic. There is little room for doubt or experimentation. We must not wait until we are actually in the fray to decide what strategies we are willing to use. We must crack the mob immediately and make the attackers fight us one at a time. Responses must be absolute and resolute.

Devastating shots for dropping your attacker include full-force shin kicks to the groin, knee strikes to the tailbone, elbow strikes to the base of the skull, and brutal head controls using the ears, hair grabs, and face gouges.

CONCLUSION

I stated at the outset that I am not a Russophile. While many of my colleagues have been motivated to immerse themselves fully in the martial culture they are studying, I have always approached my training with a very Western approach, objectively looking at the strengths and benefits of any art and taking only what serves me. The core elements of the Russian martial arts have changed my life. In these pages, I have tried to convey some small sense of the ideas and principles that have helped in this. In the end, what matters to me is that something I laid down on these pages might help you to improve the quality of your own training . . . or perhaps even save your life one day.

I invite any feedback or questions (kevinsecours@hotmail.com or www.combatsystema.com) and hope to have the honor of seeing you on the mat one day.

Training is truth.

ABOUT THE AUTHOR

Kevin Secours is an internationally known personal protection professional, specializing in the art of Russian Systema. One of the most renowned non-Russian practitioners of Russian Systema living outside Russia, Secours began training in the Russian martial arts in 1998. Known for his concise grasp of Systema and his innovative approach to sharing his knowledge, Secours has published some of the first and most comprehensive articles on the subject. In 2010, Kevin formed The International Combat Systema Association to more fully represent his continuing evolution and understanding of the Russian martial arts. His interpretation is currently practiced by more than 100 affiliates worldwide.

In addition to Systema, Secours holds a 6th-degree black belt in Goshinbudo under Sensei Sali Azem, a 3rd-degree black belt in Modern Kempo Jujitsu, a 1st-degree black belt in Akai Ryu Jiu-Jitsu, and full instructorship in Five Animal Shaolin Chuanshu. He also has more than 15 years of experience in tai chi and yoga, as well as extensive experience in the grappling arts.